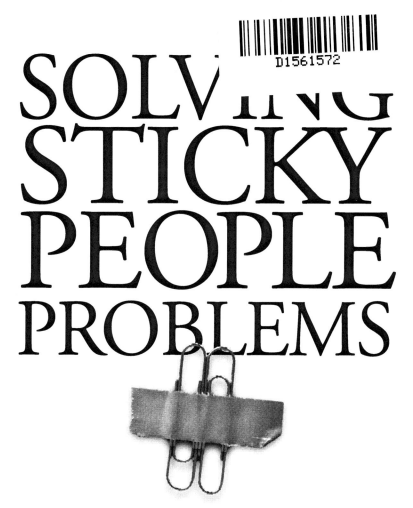

SOLVING STICKY PEOPLE PROBLEMS

USING *Your Supervisory Inner* SENSE *with* EMPLOYEES

TIM MCHEFFEY

MORGAN JAMES PUBLISHING • NEW YORK

SOLVING STICKY PEOPLE PROBLEMS

ISBN: 978-1-61448-018-1 (Paperback)
       978-1-61448-019-8 (eBook)
Library of Congress Control Number: 2011927236

Published by:
MORGAN JAMES PUBLISHING
1225 Franklin Ave Ste 32
Garden City, NY 11530-1693
Toll Free 800-485-4943
www.MorganJamesPublishing.com

Cover Photo by:
Jessica Rose Lehrman
http://studiojrose.com/

Cover/Interior Design by:
Rachel Lopez
rachel@r2cdesign.com

In an effort to support local communities, raise awareness and funds, Morgan James Publishing donates one percent of all book sales for the life of each book to Habitat for Humanity. Get involved today, visit **www.HelpHabitatForHumanity.org.**

Special thanks to my Son, Adam McHeffey who with his sage insight, created the concept for the logo design on the book cover. The rusty paperclips represent the hard-working people of the workplace… continually taping things up to keep things running as smoothly as possible. This richly captures the ongoing and worthy mission of truly solving sticky people problems.

FOREWORD

When I was a new manager early on in my career in publishing, situations arose on a daily basis that challenged me to ask myself, "How do I handle this?" From incidental issues like employees extending their 15 minute break to a half hour, to the more complex questions about how to motivate employees to perform better, to wondering what to do to help employees with personal problems that affected performance at work, to how to fire a dishonest employee. And on and on, the daily dilemma.

I was fortunate that I had a boss at that time who was a good teacher and liked discussing my daily, and sometimes more than daily, "How to handle" questions. I would stop by his office and say, "Here's the situation…what are your thoughts on how I should handle this?" His answers helped me grow as a manager to the point where I had enough experience and confidence that I could judge on my own what was the natural way for me to effectively manage people and situations.

After years of management, I arrived at the same place that Tim McHeffey does in this book. Management really is all about people. Management is a responsibility…and a privilege. We are privileged to become a part of many people's lives and families and to influence their careers and their growth as human beings. By our example, we set the standard for them against which they will learn how to interact with others in their lives and how to manage others in their own careers.

In this wonderful, punchy and to the point book, Tim McHeffey shares a simple formula for success at work and in life. PHP....purity, humility and patience. It's about treating people with respect....it's about doing unto others as you would have them to do unto you. It's about effective communication between human beings, a skill, and an art, sadly diminished in our world today.

PHP is a shortcut to management sanity...as a new manager you will read this book and think, "Is he for real? Will this work? It can't be this simple." Years from now, you will reread the book and think, "Of course, that's exactly what it's all about." This book gives you permission to be your authentic self now. It will make your management experience more effective and more enjoyable right now.

BARBARA LITRELL

BARBARA LITRELL *worked in sales and management at the New York Times, 1972-1991, served as Sr. VP Publisher of McCall's magazine 1991-1995, and President of MacDonald Communications Corp. and Group Publisher of Working Woman and Working Mother magazines 1995-2000. She then moved to Sedona, Arizona to put all her management skills to work as a community leader.*

WHAT *EXACTLY* IS A **STICKY** PEOPLE PROBLEM?!

Remember last Thursday morning…when your stomach was one big apricot pit roughing up your whole gut?! It wasn't continuous pain, but a subtle, gnawing one. You thought it might be the Tex-Mex you ate last night. Yet further consideration ushered the real culprit into view. You have that *thing* going on at work; and the more you think about it…the more you realize you're trapped. "Between a rock and a hard place," as they say. (Whenever you don't know the origin of a quote, it's always *they*. Don't try that with your teacher though!)

The gut wrenching feeling is a perceived lack of control. You're on the fence—don't know where or to whom to turn. For example, *how* are you going to tell *her*, that staring at others makes them uncomfortable? Or *where* do you start, when bringing up to *him* how his talking about guns is unnerving to fellow employees? And…what in the world do you say to your employee who smells?!

Welcome to the world of Solving **Sticky** People Problems! When you learn and use the **PHP** formula, you'll see that you really *can* handle prickly, touchy issues. Your boss will be happy (for s/he likely has little idea how to do it)…your employees will appreciate it—and you'll possibly for the first time: find a peaceful, easy feeling…knowing you did the right thing.

WHAT IS PHP, AND WHY IS IT GUARANTEED TO SOLVE STICKY PEOPLE PROBLEMS?

PHP is the most powerful ingredient in human communication. **PHP** stands for *Purity, Humility* and *Patience.* Wait, let me guess—you're thinking: oh man, here it comes…the touchy-feely stuff! Not even close! The problems that can be solved by using the **PHP** technique are hard-core, down and dirty. Keep reading, you'll see!

Purity is wholesome <u>integrity</u>, total <u>honesty</u> in mind, body and spirit. It's <u>appreciating</u> everything with <u>joy</u> and <u>enthusiasm.</u> Humility is total <u>acceptance</u> that we are small players in a big world. Ego has no place in decision-making. Confidence, yes. Ego, never. Patience is the virtue that without a doubt can make <u>all</u> <u>good</u> things possible. And patience is sort of like *waiting for further instructions.*

What does all this have to do with solving **sticky** people problems? Everything! You see, when we (Managers) are *Pure* and *Humble* and *Patient*, our thinking becomes clearer. (Note: you'll see the words APPRECIATE and ACCEPT in caps throughout the book. APPRECIATION and ACCEPTANCE are integral tools in the **PHP** process). Now, we can trust our *INNER SENSE.* We all know, deep down, what is right and wrong. All we have to do is open up our minds and listen to that genuine voice inside of all of us. The correct answers are always there. Always. I know, you're skeptical. I don't blame you. But when you apply **PHP** (as you'll read about in the upcoming pages), it'll become crystal clear to you.

This book does not contain legal advice, although **PHP** Managers tend to elude long days spent in court. The book contains "interpersonal interacting" advice. Very potent.

INTRODUCTION

U sing and "living" **PHP** is easy and basic. It's also the toughest challenge you'll encounter. You see, we know down deep— what's right and wrong. But matching those preferred behaviors to those values…well, that's a different story! It's like saying it and doing it are two different animals. So, a lot of what you'll read will be how (and why) to exercise this **PHP** stuff.

By now, you may have noticed that I write as I speak, which has become quite colloquial with many first-line supervisors and managers. Apologies in advance for any abrupt tense changes, abbreviations, grammatical indiscretions, emphatic spellings or inconsistencies. But one thing's for sure: if you treat people with respect and sincere friendliness, you get good results. It works. Totally. One hundred percent of the time. Oh yeah, sometimes in the short term, it seems like you're not getting through, or everything's getting screwed up. Well it's not really. This is where the third "P" comes in: *Patience.*

The **PHP** technique can unbelievably work to help YOU, Jane or Joe Manager—solve those sometimes excruciatingly **sticky** people problems with your employees. It'll actually work with every person you deal with. But for now, we'll concentrate on employees in work situations. Don't let the brevity fool you. Generally speaking, we business people talk too much. Simpler words and shorter conversations are most often welcomed in a work-world of complexity.

You are holding in your hot little hands right now, a hot formula: **PHP**. It has evolved over 30 plus years, and has been "road tested" across many states, occupations, and a diverse assortment of supervisors and managers for the past seven years. It works, when you let it. Utilize the ingredients willingly and gently, and allow your formidable *inner sense* to truly, finally solve your problems. Ready? Here we go!

PS. Yes, "think" is misspelled. Hopefully, it will encourage more of it (not misspelling).

PHP Managers think a whole bunch. Heaven knows we should all *thimk* more.

TABLE OF CONTENTS

SECTION A

Planning for **Sticky** *Situations—Getting Ready*

SECTION B:

Managing **Sticky** *Situations*—Day-to-Day

SECTION C

The **Sticky Challenge of Balancing**— **Work, Home and Health**…*in a world of change*

PHP MANAGER'S THEME SONG

(to the tune of "Take Me Out to the Ball Game")

I no longer get stressed out,
I now manage: o-kay;
I found the secret to help-me-out,
I don't want you to b-e left-out.
If it's hi-ring, firing, dele-ga-tion,
Or conflicts of all types…
Well it's ONE, TWO, THREE: PHP
At the Man-agement Game!

Should you sing at work? What does a silly song have to do with effectively managing employees? *Keep it light* is the message. Don't take yourself and life too seriously. This does not mean to be lazy, or to encourage it in others. It means to truly capture the heart of youth—happy, healthy, and living in the present! (You know how you *feel* when you're belting out that song on your car radio on your way to work? Bring that same *spirit* into work with you). Be yourself.

SECTION A

Planning for **Sticky Situations**
—Getting Ready—

Chapter 1

A Word About Goals (in a Sticky World)

How to find what you really want.

*Setting goals is important, but **resetting** is vital!*

NOTES FROM THE PHP MANAGER'S JOURNAL...

"The faith one has in him/herself comes from the faith one has in God. He is the one who will use us (as we will allow) for the good of others; which is ultimately for the good of us."

—EILEEN MCPHELLIN, *Director of Religious Formation, St. Rosalie's Parish, Hampton Bays, NY; and Store Manager, World Village Fair Trade Market (all volunteer-run retail store)*

"Writing goals? Who the H-E-double hockey sticks has time for that?!"

—JG

"Our past designs us but does not define us."

—CATHY O'BRIEN, *"Cathy's Garden"*

STICKY NEWS
EXTRA, EXTRA, READ ALL ABOUT IT!

Self-Manager Runs Out of Energy?!

The manager began her day calmly. She subscribed to The One-Minute Manager suggestion to "enter the day more slowly." Had a healthy breakfast and was feeling steady before the board members to whom she was to present (kind of felt like Derek Jeter at Short). Presentation went well. Then at lunch, the waiter tipped her tensions a bit when she least expected it. He probably didn't mean to drip on her new wool jacket, and it was just water…but it pushed her buttons just the same. She promised herself she would not let the little things in life trouble her (easier said than done).

The rest of her day went well—status quo, except for that one phone call from her rear-end of a client. But she expected it from *him*. She was braced, stanchioned, ready (remember, like Derek?). The day ended without further incident. The 30-something manager arrived home to her typical American domicile scenario including a hubby, two teeny-boppers and a dog. Post dinner, she had four hours 'til her favorite sitcom rerun came on; lots of time to catch up on mail correspondence, laundry, cleaning the den, and finishing painting the bathroom trim. But she did…nothing. For she was spent. Wiped!

We've had it all wrong for decades. The pie of life is not time, but energy. When we're prepared for things to go awry during the normal course of the day, we renew energy. When we're not prepared for distracting, harmful occurrences (albeit seemingly small), we loose energy like a vacuum—sucked right out of us! Result: those four hours are spent unproductively. It's okay to relax on the sofa in front of the tube *if* it's okay with *you!* Here's the point: when all those "someday I'll" chores add up undone, the mental strain creates an additional energy drain. Ruts become the next phase in the disheartening process.

We must be keenly aware of **energy**. It's a precious, golden asset—to be nurtured. Awareness alone goes a long way to sustaining it. The "pie" of our lives is not slices of time. That's easy. Energy is the ingredient to be savored and APPRECIATED, for then—it gets renewed, and even increased.

WHY GOAL SETTING DOES NOT WORK

We attend workshops on writing goals. We visualize, we plan, and we get excited. Then, *when* things don't work out as planned, we take the nine hand-written pages of life strategy over which we grueled, and toss them into the bottom drawer. And we quietly utter that goal setting doesn't work. Goal setting *is* important. But only because it's a segue to goal *resetting*. Life does not work. Stuff breaks. Things do not go "on plan." **PHP** Managers work like heck to organize and schedule efficiently and effectively, but realize we are not in full control of the full sequence of life events (**HUMILITY**). **PHP** Managers perpetually adapt. The "new way" is usually better. **PHP**ers ACCEPT resetting, retooling, refocusing as bona-fide tools of managing. *Expect* it. Much easier that way.

What could possibly be sticky in goal setting? Your new employee comes on and appears to be a very strong addition to your team. But from her first week, she says how she'll "be running this place someday soon!" She also tosses in how women are better visionaries then men—and she'll "be taking full advantage of that quality" in herself. Should you:

A. Advise her it's okay to have high aspirations, but to keep them to herself? Just to keep to her job description for now?

B. Promote her as fast as you can? Tell your boss you've got a real go-getter here? Do anything you can to keep her around?

C. Advise her to keep very conscious of rubbing her fellow employees the wrong way?

Sticky people problem solving managers help their employees use **PHP** as well. Here's how one supervisor took all of the above into consideration. Check out this hybridized answer and how it embraces **PHP**.

MANAGER: "Hi, Ali. Before the day ends, I'd like us to chat for a few about your future. Now's probably as good a time as any (Ali motions affirmatively). You have high aspirations. That's great. Keep that enthusiastic energy flowing. And thank you for continuing to keep *me* updated on where you'd like your career to go and so on. I'm excited for you, and keeping the communication alive helps *us* to plan as well as a company (**PURITY**). Along with that, I have two requests for you. They're actually more like suggestions. The first is to be patient with your ambitions; patient with us here at the firm in helping you to get where you want to be. We move quicker than many employers—but it still may not seem fast enough for you. And also, be patient with yourself. Be deliberate and keep thinking things through—and you'll be wildly successful. But calm endurance (**PATIENCE**) adds enjoyment to the process. So far, so good, Ali?"

ALI: "Yup, all sounds good!"

MANAGER: "Great. The second recommendation is to keep your *going up* goals to yourself. Except for me as your supervisor and maybe close family members, don't tell anyone. There's an expression which tells us never to complain; because 80 percent of the people don't care, and the other 20 percent are glad we have the problems we do. The other reason is that many, many people are jealous. JFK said that jealousy has killed more people than cancer. When you share ambitious goals with your peers, they'll often feel badly; maybe even mad and resentful that you have *something going on* which they don't. It's not fair but it's real. An effective leader (both present and future) needs to have the respect and likability of all people. If other employees like you, you'll get promoted faster in a good company. It's a fact of life."

ALI: "So I should hold myself back?"

MANAGER: "On the contrary. But it's *how* you propel yourself forward. I'm telling you to be very conscious of *everyone's* feelings along your career ladder—both your peers and those to whom you're responsible (***HUMILITY***). Sincerely keep that in mind, be honest with all matters (***PURITY***), and hang in there (***PATIENCE***). Doing these things is about the most control you'll ever have—because your inner sense will be guiding your every move—day to day."

Did it work? You really don't know yet. But it doesn't matter. Read on.

Chapter 2

Planning
Smooth Schedules

How to use this tool for minimum **stickiness** *and maximum efficiency. And make all your employees happy!*

NOTES FROM THE PHP MANAGER'S JOURNAL...

"I have a scheduling calendar. The employees write all the times they *can't work*. No reasons, just times. In 38 years and dozens of workers, we've *never* had a problem working it out. I tell 'em all when they start that *it just works*. And *they* make it work. And it does."

—BEN M. *(small business owner, seven-day retail operation)*

STICKY NEWS

EXTRA, EXTRA, READ ALL ABOUT IT!

Boss' Daughter's Friend Makes "Her Own Schedule!"

Just treat her like everyone else your boss directed. *No special treatment.* Uh huh. Okay, you've got the *responsibility* of scheduling. Your boss has given you the *authority* to carry out that responsibility. But you still think you have to keep *her* happy. **PHP** Clarification: You do, but make that—you have to keep *everyone* happy. What, too soft for you?! Bottom line: happy employees will generally translate into productive work environments (including satisfied customers— both internal and external).

So how does a manager keep employees gleeful? The main ingredient any mortal longs for is *fairness and consistency.* Believe it or not, it's all the boss' daughter's friend wants as well. In the old days (whatever that means), supervisors would make variable work schedules. Employees would work the hours without debate. End of story. In the current "two to three jobs per person economy," some additional flexibility is in order—IF we desire a smoother running workplace. It used to be a simple science—we had *hours* or lack of hanging over their heads. Now it's more of an art form; *communication art* to be precise...hence, **PHP**.

Elik is likely the most valuable part-timer in your branch of the city public library. His title is "shelf clerk" which means he checks out materials for patrons (he's the quickest and most friendly), and reshelves books in the down time (faster and more accurately than the rest). But he also answers the phones, and helps inquiring patrons as competently as most educated research librarians. The problem? He unremittingly requests his co-workers to switch work times with him on the schedule. He always seems to have somewhere else to be—jobs, social, charity work. Elik's a busy dude (he's also the one you ask to get those special projects *done*, because he does).

Courtney has been grousing on the old grapevine how Elik's "favors" are annoying. "He should just work his friggin' schedule like the rest of us do," was passed onto you. What Courtney does not know is that months ago, Elik asked if *you* thought he should attempt to juggle his other jobs with the library schedule, or just give his notice to you. Because you didn't want to lose such a fine employee, you inferred it could all be worked out with juggling. Do you:

A. Ask Courtney about her grumblings—get it all out in the open?

B. Do nothing? (There's no problem here).

C. Send Elik to smooth it out with Courtney?

D. Bring up scheduling at the next staff meeting?

E. Advise Elik it's time to reprioritize and maybe quit?

F. Ask your dog, Sarge, how to proceed?

G. Ask Courtney and Elik what to do?

　　Some thoughts on the choices...

A. Never ask a question you pretty surely know the answer to, but may catch someone in a lie. IOW, she probably grumbled. If you put her in an embarrassing position, she may feel compelled to stretch the truth. Don't ask.

B. The rule is, if at least one employee isn't operating 100 percent for whatever reason, consider addressing the issue.

C. This could seem like it could really work. He's a charmer. She caves. Façade is: problem solved—but it's just been veneered for the moment. This is simply prolonging the problem and perhaps even deepening it.

D. Maybe. But waaay too much is brought up at meetings when it's authentically an individual issue.

E. You're not smart enough to reach this conclusion (choosing "E" would be depending way too much on your own controlling, managing ego).

F. Good idea. Maybe just hearing yourself pose the question out loud will jostle the answer process. And Sarge will enjoy the attention.

G. MBO (managing by objectives) says first to agree on the final goal, the objective. In this case, for Elik to work out augmented schedules, and for Courtney and the others to not be annoyed by it. The next step is for everyone involved to have some say, some part in the solution. No one individual (including the manager) knows the exact solution...*before* MBO is properly utilized. "G" is a valid option. Ask them individually: how to fix this? Be **PURE**, giving as much detail as needed to both parties (but preserving the anonymity of how you discovered the problem—and tell them both *why* you're protecting the un-named). Be **HUMBLE** by confessing to them that you don't have a handle on the best way to address this. Be **PATIENT** with any potential solutions which may be presented. Remember, you asked.

For instance, what if Courtney says there should be no changes after the schedule is posted. This is not realistic in this day and age. Oh sure, you can be a manager- tough-guy and insist...but you're creating a work world of mediocrity—for fabricated excuses will flourish and absences will increase (yes, statistically true). And guaranteed, the Courtneys of the world won't be happy then either.

SO WHAT HAPPENS WHEN MBO BACKFIRES?

You may have to take the reins at this point. In this case, the actual **PHP** Manager changed the policy to have all changes go through him.

Some interesting outcomes blossomed. Courtney and crew seemed to enjoy being "managed" more (maybe scheduling should not have been delegated to "group-think" in the first place?). And/or maybe she had less reason to be jealous of Elik with his busier, more active lifestyle. And Elik became what appeared to be more organized about his entire life! What exactly made him a better planner is still unknown, but the fact remains he was able to function with less juggling. And they lived happily ever after.

Sounds too easy? Keep reading; we're just warming up.

PROPER GOAL-SETTING
SHOULD FEEL LIKE...

A Hundred and One Things that Feel Good!

 # 14: "Prom day is big when you're 17. Busy day coming up— test at school, short shift at your part-time job, hair appointment... then staying up all night. Exciting, but scary; as you're one of those who needs your eight hours. But you're tossing and turning the night before. OMG, you leap up, your clock says 8:00 AM—you've overslept by two hours! Wait...your eyes adjust; it says 2:00 AM. Four more hours of heavenly sleep in front of you. What a feeling as you crawl back into that warm, comfy den of fluffy pillows and comforter. Mmmm...sweet dreams!"

Chapter 3

Keeping High Quality/ High *Productivity*/ High Morale

Help your employees to **destickyize** *their own work —high performance will result!*

NOTES FROM THE PHP MANAGER'S JOURNAL...

"Yeah, okay—I buy into the whole quality thing and taking great care of customers, but passing it onto my employees is a perpetual

13

task. Regularly, we need to show employees *what's in it for them* in *money, perks and time. That's what everyone wants.* I call it MPT."

—ANONYMOUS *(kept this way cause I even have to massage my boss using MPT too; he wouldn't like it if he read I did that!)*

"I'll be here for awhile, miss. I'm getting paid by the hour."

—OIL BURNER TECHNICIAN

"I am a firm believer in the Five M's – Mentor, Motivate, Manage, Monitor and Measure, (I think there is a 6th – an M word for reward, I do that, just can't remember the word). Anyway this has worked pretty well for me over the past years." (Could she be thinking of M&Ms?!)

—EILEEN LIA, *Medical Billing Executive*

STICKY NEWS
EXTRA, EXTRA, READ ALL ABOUT IT!

Big Mouth Millie – vs. – Plain Jane!

Big Mouth Millie is at it again…telling whoever will listen how she's the best salesperson in the universe. And that's okay to a point. At least she's excited about something, and takes lots of pride and ownership in the store (more than can be said about many employees).

Really starts becoming a problem when she compares herself with fellow-salesperson, Jane though. Millie tells her right to her face, "We gotta' light a fire under you girl!" Jane simply ushers in her typical, quiet smile. Customers seem to like Jane, and she always appears to be working with customers; she just doesn't seem to maintain Millie's criteria for how to be "on the floor."

Millie pays no attention to sales figures—not her own, nor the store's. Never has in her 28-year career. "Who needs stats when my customers keep coming in year after year?" is her chant. Millie's thing is: if you're excited to sell, and there are people on the floor, well there you go…all is well!

But time goes by as it always does, and conversations about *the economy* increase. And surprise, Millie's quarterly productivity report is down; specifically her *sales-per-hour* and her *average sale* numbers. And perhaps the most important statistic is the one which measures something called "personal selling cost." It's how much Millie *sells* per hour, compared to what she is *paid* per hour. And it's way out of whack. The years have been kind to her in terms of annual increases. So presently, she simply costs too much for the amount she's moving out the door. Jane's numbers however, are all excellent.

As you're preparing for annual reviews, you need to bring items of concern to the attention of your employees. In your informal "prep chat" with Millie, do you:

A. Just post the figures on the bulletin board in the lounge?

B. Just wait for the official review?

C. Publicly proclaim Jane's numbers, and explain to the whole group *why* they are so good?

D. Ask Millie to give some sales tips at the next store meeting?

E. Bake some brownies and bring them into work? (Everything goes better with brownies).

F. Show Jane's numbers to Millie, and her own as well?

G. Quit your job as manager? (Big-Mouth-Millie will eat you alive!)

H. Show Millie her numbers for the quarter, and how they compare with the averages for the store?

Some thoughts on the answer choices…

A. Just post in the lounge: ah yes, peer pressure—we all know it well. Does it work? Sure. Would posting work? Probably. It would likely result in a competitive environment, perhaps more intense for the smooth workplace you're used to though. Employees do better when they are relaxed; on their toes, yes—but not looking over their shoulders to see who may be back-biting.

B. Just wait for review time? Verrry common. It's a copout though, or a scapegoat. This may seem appealing because it lets us breathe a bit more, before we have to face the issue. It's like the longer you stay in the warm water of the heated pool on a cool fall evening, the tougher it is to get out. Bottom line: the longer we put it off, the tougher to handle for all parties.

C. Put Jane on the pedestal? Maybe. But you still won't solve the problem. Millie will have no idea where you're coming from.

D. You will never have to *ask* Millie to share tips!

E. Can't hurt. It's generally true that everything goes better with brownies.

F. Millie does not have (what HR folks call) a *need to know* Jane's numbers. But we're getting warm…

G. Quit? It's always an option, but hang in there, you'll be boarding the **PHP** train momentarily.

H. Millie should see her quarterly stats. And assuming there are more than two salespeople in the store, she *should* see the averages as well. Anonymity will be maintained, and she will see how she stacks up (or down in this case). Like door nails and dead men, numbers don't lie. From this point on,

Millie will simply fly right…or out. Sounds simple, right?! Let's take a stab at the potential conversation…

MANAGER: "Hi, Millie, thanks for coming in. Millie, I think you're the best salesperson here. You sell better than anyone else…" sscchheeuaaeeikkkk!! (that's the sound of a DJ stopping a spinning record—you know, when the whole party comes to a dead hush? What, you have a better way to spell that sound?!)

Where the heck is the **PURITY** in that? It ain't true, dude! And the throwing in the "I think," is scapegoating…like what you're about to tell is what *someone else* thinks, like your boss or the "company" or something. You're protecting your ego. That behavior lacks **HUMILITY**. Maybe, just maybe let's try being **PATIENT** with ourselves first—like, begin conversing honestly. Something like…

MANAGER: "Hi, Millie, thanks for coming in. Millie, I need to share something with you—and I'm not quite sure how to do it."

MILLIE: "Well you know that you can always share with me. We've been friends far too long to *not* be able to."

MANAGER: "It's like sometimes when employees are talking on the sales floor, they talk about things—"

MILLIE: (Interrupting) "I think I know where this is going."

MANAGER: (Hopefully) "You do?"

MILLIE: "The rumors traveling around about you and little Janey-girl having a little tot-a-tot."

MANAGER: "Huh?"

MILLIE: "Don't you worry about it. I told them all. What he does is *his* business!"

Let's analyze so far. The way it began resulted in Millie thinking it had *nothing* to do with her. *Then* it became very distracting for the manager when Millie threw him the screwball about his (grapevine) affair.

THIMK! *Whenever something is <u>not</u> going smoothly, just pause and begin again. It's almost like the use of* **PHP** *is <u>renewed</u> during the conversation. You'll naturally become stronger.*

MANAGER: "Wait, no, Millie. This isn't going to the way it's supposed to be. Let me rewind and start again. The fact is that despite the fact that you're one of the most popular, spirited people working here, your sales numbers need some help. Let me please show you what I mean. (Short pause for a breath). When I say spirited, Millie, I mean it's great to have you there. You're a beacon of enthusiasm to the other salespeople *(PURITY).* That's why I hope I deliver this the right way *(HUMILITY).* And it's all in the name of simply making *everything* work even better. (Brief glance of eye contact to make sure Millie is still *in the conversation).* Your *sales-per-hour* are almost exactly average with the rest of the store. This is not bad, because you work weekdays and most of the business is done percentage-wise on nights and weekends. So when you're there, you're selling. (Millie nods like *darn right!).* (*PATIENCE* is exhibited here as the manager just keeps focusing on the message). Your *average sale* is just slightly below the store average. Could also have to do with your *day* shift, again as opposed to nights and weeken…"(Millie interrupts).

MILLIE: "I signed on for Monday through Friday years ago."

ACTION BRIEF! PATIENCE *uses one's "pass the butter" voice—natural and non-emotional.*

MANAGER: "And I'm not suggesting you change that, Millie. I'm just explaining *why* these figures look the way they do. Just to take the conversation to the next level though, if you did put in a night and/or weekend day, you'd likely see a jump in those productivity numbers."

MILLIE: "Then who would clean the store like I do when it slows down in the afternoon? You think those young princesses will? Hah! Too busy talking to their little prima-donna boyfriends!"

(**MANAGER** pauses, not knowing how if at all to address that statement).

ACTION BRIEF! *PAUSE. "Say nothing," Grandma said, "if you have nothing good to say." Good advice. Pauses are an excellent form of communication.*

MANAGER: (Deciding simply to continue). "The last statistic we look at, Millie, is possibly the most important, as it truly looks at everyone individually. It's called selling cost. Picture two pots of money. One is your salary, say, per week. The other is the amount which you *sell* in that same week. When we ratio the two together, we get a percentage. From a profitability standpoint, the lower—the better."

(**PHP** Manager's Bonus Tip: actually drawing illustrations helps people understand. A picture is often worth a million words).

MILLIE: (Seemingly interested) "The lower, the better?"

MANAGER: "Right. A low selling cost means it costs the store *less* to sell a certain amount of goods. Here's yours compared to the store average." (Clearly shows that Millie's numbers are relatively *un*-productive).

MILLIE: "So we all must be down with the bad economy, huh?"

(**PHP** Manager's "thought bubble echoing above your head" is now saying "holy cow, how does such a stupid person even get through life?!" But the manager circles the **PHP** wagons yet again); *(PATIENCE).*

MANAGER: "Well, yeah. That's all part of it, Millie. But let me just try to explain it a little clearer. I know it's complicated at first, but it's important—so just stay with me on this."

(Still using the neutral *please pass the butter voice*). "Many people don't quite get it the first time, including me actually *(HUMILITY)*. And once it does make sense to you, it will help you, and the store and me." *(PURITY)*.

Millie will listen more focusedly, for she knows you're on her side. And a big thing *you've* got going on here is that *you care*—about her, the company, the quality of your job, your work. And she does too! A **PHP** atmosphere nurtures this *I really <u>do</u> give a flying fish* attitude! Once Millie understands, truly gets it (and this will occur by your explaining it as many times as it takes *(PATIENCE), she* will become the powerful lever on the sales floor, even explaining the concept to the others. You're helping her do: what she naturally does best. You're riding the horse in the direction it's already going. You're keeping the round peg in the round hole. Blah, blah, blah—you get the picture.

HOW TO STAY FOCUSED IN A WORLD OF EMPLOYEE DISTRACTIONS

Employees scapegpoat. They try to throw us off. It's a natural defense mechanism. For example, when Millie reminded her manager they were long-time "friends." It's challenging to work with someone everyday for years—and not develop some type of friendship. Fact is, **PHP** Managers *naturally* have safe **PHP** friendships. Without hidden agendas and pretentious pedestals, a smooth communication flow naturally grows. It sounds so easy. But it is. **PHP** working relationships grow as an Oak tree thickens into trustworthy strength—quietly, but surely.

Employees will often compare themselves to others as a means of taking the light off themselves. **PHP** Managers simply do *not* engage in this distraction, by remaining focused on the topic at hand: that present, particular employee's situation.

How about being accused of having an affair?! The manager had a clear choice. Engage in the topic, perhaps defending himself with denial… orrrr just move on—not giving it any energy at all. If you're a human manager (likely), you know this is easier said than done. But assuming you're **PURE** in all your dealings, "The truth will set you free." Meaning it really is okay just to move on. Tawdry rumors often disappear without the fuel of cheap talk.

A manager can also be distracted by his/her own need for *control.* The MBO technique (managing by objectives) means for everyone, manager and employees, to clarify the objectives/goals/what needs to be accomplished. And then *all* work together to get it done. Employees often know better methods to success than we do. Swallow a little controlling pride and ask them. They will naturally take greater *ownership* in the decision and the outcome. It's an inherent, human desire to help, and do well…and to work up to one's potential. Their natural WIIFMs (what's in it for me) will shine through.

Consider the alternative of the above technique. They wait for you to tell them every little, stinkin' detail of what to do, when to do it, and how. Sure, you'll feel wanted. But soon you'll learn a tenet of **PHP** delegation: the place should run even *better* when the **PHP** Manager is not there. Further and more importantly, it's not natural for great employees to feel low morale.

ACTION BRIEF! Let them think! This begins a domino effect where the quality of their work habits heightens. Morale will take care of itself.

Do the above action brief and there'll be less employees waiting for five o'clock on Fridays to come around. Good employees want to do the right thing. So how do you, **PHP** Manager give them the slack they need to take care of their own productivity in performing quality work? One effective technique is to use what some managers call the "critical path," AKA the worst possible case. This does not mean being a poopy Peter or Paula—dooming and glooming. It just means fully understanding what is the very worst outcome (on a project you might delegate, for instance)…and then working like heck to make sure it does not happen. **PHP** Managers are the ultimate clean-up batters, hitting number four in the life line-up; behind our employees, our customers, our families. We are paid well—to fix other peoples' problems.

One more distraction: what about the employee for example, who complains how everyone else is a slob at work…no one eeeeever puts things away and so on. He or she will be the one chanting, "Without me, this whole place would stop functioning—because no one could find anything!" First, you may wish to *thank them*. That's right. Simple acknowledgment of how you appreciate their extra efforts (without the fear of them asking for a raise), goes a mile! If you're feeling really bravely-delegative (made-up phrase?!), you may even give them some tips of how *they* can help *you*: to help along the issue. Instead of them continuing becoming POed—tossing things around all huffy, they might try reminding their fellow (sloppy) co-workers about first impressions. And that when merchandise and supplies are returned to their proper places, it's more convenient for *everyone*.

(Note to **PHP** Self: wouldn't it be nice if everyone and everything just worked together like an old grandfather clock, with little involvement from you?!)

TOTAL QUALITY MANAGEMENT, THE MALCOLM BALDRIDGE AWARD, AND JOHNNY'S BUTCHER SHOP

Saturday mornings for a certain youngster meant a trip to Johnny's, for the finest cuts of meat for the family dinner that evening. The young boy will never forget Johnny's face when the boy's mom confessed last week's roast was okay, but it wasn't "Johnny."

Well, Johnny could not define TQM but he sure could serve it up. No charge that week for the new one, of course…*and* a phone call to see how the new one was cooking up so far; and, *and!* who's at the door at dessert time, hot apple pie in hand? You guessed it. Johnny!

The visual in the youngster's memory remains potently some forty years later. As the adults were shooting the breeze over coffee (and pie, of course), he thought, "Would she ever go anywhere else for her meat?" He also recalled those high numbers coming up on that old, brown, cash register. Price was *never* an object; never even discussed!

TQM (total quality management) is doing it right the first time; and taking care of screw-ups when they occur—quickly and completely. TQM should also be a habit in everything we do. The ISO9000 series (International Standard for Organization) and "Six Sigma" are processes for management to reach and maintain quality standards. Some companies apply for and win the prestigious Malcolm Baldridge award for quality. A funny thing sometimes occurs after the prize however. They start slacking—giving crumby service, bum products. Makes you wonder whether they really gave a flying fish in the first place?

Johnny cared. He consistently *did it right the first time.* When a task is not completed properly, it comes back haunting—costing more time and money to fix the problem. Remember the guys who built your large deck? You actually saw them "measure twice and cut once." The additional care they maintained within the process shortened the length of the job incredibly. Their boss was happy because their dollars per hour earned were quite high. You were happy because the job was finished. You were barbequing within a week! "They were worth it," you boasted to your friends. PS. And you didn't find one cigarette butt around afterwards.

The real goal of this chapter is to *believe* that we really can make work life better for employees. Then in turn, they can make their home lives better; for themselves and everyone they touch. "Johnny-Managing" the process of quality makes for excellent and consistent products and smooth, effective services.

ACTION BRIEF! *Do the right thing! Even when those around you, above and below you…do not.*

Make things with pride. Serve your external and internal customers well. You'll rapidly develop a reputation of trust. You'll never have to look over your shoulder. That's a high-octane feeling of pleasure. Positively energizing!

PROPERLY MANAGING <u>PRODUCTIVITY</u>
SHOULD FEEL LIKE...

A Hundred and One Things that Feel Good!

 # 12: *"Seems like you've been driving behind this truck for hours... you're not sure which is more annoying, the smelly black smoke from the exhaust or the fact that he's moving at the pace of a millepede! Gas, brake. Gas, brake. Uhh! And then, there it is: TWO LANES! You look in the mirrors, and make the break! Accelerating past the giant double trailer was freeing—exhilarating!"*

Chapter 4

(How Not to Get Stuck When) *Recruiting* and *Hiring*

Finding, hiring and keeping winners!

NOTES FROM THE PHP MANAGER'S JOURNAL...

"I think a good manager is one who really allows an employee/ direct report to flourish. Some the attributes that come to mind for a high achieving employee (are that) they are intelligent, work independently, are humble in that they know how to ask the right questions and seek advice when needed but do not need to be

25

micromanaged. If you want independence you can't micromanage, if you want thoughtfulness through good questions etc., you can't slam someone for asking a dumb question etc. And so, two quotes come to mind: 'Treat people as if they were what they ought to be and you help them to become what they are capable of being.' - Johann W. von Goethe. And another on heavy-handed management essentially through fear, 'I would rather try to persuade a man to go along, because once I have persuaded him, he will stick. If I scare him, he will stay just as long as he is scared, and then he is gone.' – Dwight D. Eisenhower."

—DR. JEFF HAGER, *Scientist/ Director of Biology, Aragon Pharmaceuticals, Inc. San Diego, CA*

STICKY NEWS
EXTRA, EXTRA, READ ALL ABOUT IT!

Great Employee Caught In An Old Lie!

You've done it! 'Went and hired yourself a winner! He's worked beautifully now for six weeks, and you can't believe how quickly he catches on.

How he takes initiative...truly a gift from God! And then it comes to your attention that he lied on his application (and in his interview with you). We're not talking a couple months or even a couple years—but a full ten years! He wrote and said 2003, but the reference check came back with 1993. Do you:

A. Can his sorry butt, a lie's a lie? Besides, it's policy. And you must be fair and consistent.

B. Ask him why (leaving yourself open to another potential, untrue excuse)?

C. Just let the dust settle (for as long as possible)? After all, he's doing fine in his work.

Read this dialogue and decide for yourself how effective you think it is.

MANAGER: (Visibly heated) "Ah, Don, I just got some very disturbing news from HR. You may think you can fool some others, but let me assure you pal: it's not my first day at the rodeo!"

DON (Employee): (Visibly confused) "I'm not really sure what you mean?"

MANAGER: (Louder) "Don't you dare pull that crap with me! You knew damn well when you lied on your application, that you thought you could pull a fast one on me…ten years off your graduation date! You were trying to hide your age, and didn't have the @*^%^# to be up front about it! Do you have any idea how this makes me look?! You even snowed me into almost recommending you for a promotion!"

DON: (Quietly, remorsefully) "There's a reason…"

THIMK! *Is it (whatever it is) really a problem? This question will always have the same knee-jerk answer: it depends. <u>Everything</u> is <u>always</u> contingent on the situation.*

MANAGER: (Butting in quickly, noticeably upset, voice shaking) "There's no reason for anything! Now if you're smart, Don, if that's even your name, you'll get the ^&%$# out of here, so I can begin to put back the pieces of my crumbling department!" (Manager walks out).

A few comments/questions/thoughts…did the manager APPRECIATE *anything* about the six good weeks that Don had given to the company? Did the manager's ego get in the way of her sound decision-making? Did she exercise the virtue of patience?! Is the problem solved?

How does Don feel?

How does the manager feel?!

First off, is it really a problem? This initial thinking process also prompts questions, like in Don's case: did he do it intentionally? Well in this case, that's an easy one to answer. It's not like it's a misprint—it's a full three digits off! So now you're thinking, it depends on *what?*

ACTION BRIEF! Jump to NO conclusions.

Enter the use of the tool: **PHP.** Let's take it through the process, shall we?

First, *PURITY.* You want to believe that there's a darn good reason that Don wrote it. You want to trust that in his integrity process that he came to a good conclusion. You want to jump to no conclusions, and at least APPRECIATE that his cognitive direction was pure…on the right track; though at this point, you do not know why.

Now, be *HUMBLE* in ACCEPTING the fact that you have a problem. Yes. It is your problem. You hired the clown (oops, there I go—letting my ego get in the way…blaming others). It is *always* the manager's responsibility. No scapegoating allowed. ACCEPT the fact that you (big-man manager or big-lady manager) may have screwed up…'hired a liar. Now, fear starts creeping in,

"What else has he lied about…is he hosing me on other things too—ripping off the company??!!"

Relax, here's where *PATIENCE* comes in. Now, you have the full **PHP** arsenal working for you. You can't go wrong. It's not possible! Patience, first and foremost, has to be applied to yourself. Be patient with the idea that all this is happening for a reason, and don't try to rush through it. Many managers do rush, thinking these are minor items not worthy of thought. But they are.

Particularly in this case, you're dealing with a person who has, in a very short time, gained lots of favor as an excellent and contributing employee. This type does not grow on trees (not in this climate, that is!). And be sure to extend patience to your employee as well, especially when you're checking into the situation.

Now, let's try it again, this time using **PHP.**

MANAGER: (Soft spoken, neutral tone) "Don, I need to ask you about something that HR brought to my attention this morning."

DON: "What's that?"

MANAGER: "In the routine reference checking process, the date of your degree came back 1993, and not 2003 as was stated on your application. I actually went back to my interview notes, and it was stated as 2003 during our initial conversation. I'm hoping there's some confusion that can be easily cleared up?"

DON: (Pauses, appears upset, almost teary-eyed) "I…I'm sorry. I lied. I'll just leave now. I'm really sorry. 'Hope I didn't cause you too much…" (Begins to rise).

MANAGER: "Why, Don? What was your reason?" (Using same, neutral voice).

DON: "Does it really matter now?"

MANAGER: "I don't know?"

DON: "I was talking to my neighbor the morning of my interview with you. Told him this was my dream job. He told me my degree was too dated for this field, and to just say that it was more recent. I knew it was wrong when he said it, and when I wrote it; and have thought about it every single day since I've been here. I feel so stupid right now. I'm really very sorry. You've been the best boss I've ever had. (Pause for both parties). I guess that's it, right?"

MANAGER: "I'm not sure. Is there anything else I should know, about anything?"

DON: "No, that's it. Just that I never meant to put you in any kind of position like this. And I know I'll be leaving now, but I want you to know that you've been great, and so is this company. I really screwed myself."

MANAGER: "It is true, Don, that the policy does say that any false statement on the app is grounds for immediate dismissal. And I'm not sure that anything can be done, nor am I even sure how I feel personally. But before we close this conversation, let me discuss your reasoning with the higher-ups. Again, I'm not sure what difference it'll even make, but let me just make sure. I'll get back to you within the hour."

Now what?! He's a banner employee! But you know that you legally and ethically have to be fair and consistent. Did he have a good reason for exercising his lack of integrity? Can you (or more importantly, your company) forgive Don's actions? In other words, can you APPRECIATE *(PURITY)* from where he was coming? Or doesn't it matter? What if he were the "somewhat close cousin of your father-in-law?" Would most reasonable employees agree with your decision? Because even though it's confidential, pretend they'll still find out.

Can you ACCEPT (with *HUMILITY*) that everybody makes mistakes? Or not? Why does HR have a lag time, you ask? And also, how big was the mistake? How much will it impact everyone? Is the *PATIENCE* you're exhibiting just being whimpy? Or is it time and energy well spent?

The three short paragraphs above comprise the process of using **PHP**. WHEN, yes, when, and only when you are in this predicament, the answers will absolutely come to you. It's not easy. In fact it's downright draining: answering the above questions—coming up with a solution to the Don situation. But it will come; bank on that.

PURE thinking will always give rise to fully APPRECIATING how the employee is thinking, and how you should be thinking as well. *HUMBLE* actions will let you ACCEPT completely: the entire slate of details, without your ego muddying the situation. And that ever-important dose of *PATIENCE* will always keep managers from having to decide too quickly, before complete analysis of the whole picture can take place. Situations are best looked at from all sides, all angles. We already *have* the right answers inside all of us. This process *allows* them to flow out easily. And the solutions are always correct. 'Guaranteed.

THE PHP MANAGER IS
A PERPETUAL RECRUITER

Do you ever wonder why some **PHP** Managers have seemingly no trouble finding employees, while others always have gaps? Wait, stop. Just think about that for a moment. Some companies are always at full capacity; others advertise continuously and have the perennial help-wanted sign in the window. You'll read in Chapter Seven how it has very little to do with salary, company gyms, and bottomless cups of coffee.

PHP Managers are recruiting experts (taking nothing away from terrific HR departments). They are *experts*, because **PHP** Managers *get*: that recruiting is a continuous task—especially when there are no present openings. Here's how it can work…good communicators (like you, **PHP** Manager) *engage* people—all people! **PHP** communicators ask questions, because they really want to know.

They're interested. They genuinely enjoy others. During the course of various social conversations, **PHP** Managers engage others in discussions. When you ask others about themselves (work, school, kids, etc.), they generally enjoy the subject. 'Important **PHP** rule to remember: this is *not* a job interview! In fact, some of the social questions you're tossing could be considered discriminatory—causing potential legal problems. For instance, in almost any job, there's never a bona-fide reason to ask anyone if they have kids. You're just chatting. If *he* says he used to do *this* kind of job, you could possibly say, "Oh, we hire people to do that at our company," or "We do something similar at our firm." In another case, if *she* says her cousin is looking for *that* kind of job…why, you may be able to direct her to a colleague of yours (or maybe *you* can even use her!).

Networking is a much over-used word, sometimes bearing negative connotations as well. The "working-the-room" techniques are gone however (or should be). **PHP** networking is not "pulling strings," it's simply **P**eople **H**elping **P**eople. It's a wonderful cycle.

The **PHP** Manager enjoys talking about work—their own, and others. Future employees should not be searched out or wished for. The **PHP** networking techniques will open subtle recruiting doors—like divine accidents. It is casting your net across part of the universe. The net..."works" itself; building and strengthening like one of those big, beautiful summer spider webs (much of which you can't even see!). *You never know from where your next great employee is coming.* But living and breathing the aforementioned methods, will insure you'll have a steady flow. It's kind of a neat coincidence that **PHP** is also the acronym for the appropriate...*people helping people.* But we should remain mindful what it means to infuse **PHP** into recruiting and hiring. *PURITY* applied here, is enthusiastically APPRECIATING conversing with others. *HUMILITY* may be honestly sharing with them that it *is* sometimes challenging to find good, happy employees. That's why you take the opportunity to chat with others. And *PATIENCE* is simply believing that it will happen. When some **PHP** Managers hear of this technique, they think, "But I'm not in sales, I can't be pushy." All you're doing is making human connections—people helping people.

In another common predicament, your employee wants you to hire her (long-time, close) cousin, and you don't want to. 'Just doesn't feel like a fit. Try the **PHP** approach...*with the cousin:* "Hi, Roger, it's good to meet you. My name is **PHP** Manager. Your cousin, Helen, mentioned that you might be interested in working with us here at O'Sullivan Bros. Lumber Company. (Roger may or may not elaborate here, nor does it matter). When looking at the positions available, and your background, I'm a bit surprised you're interested.

Generally, we look for someone who has been involved in a similar line of work. So, I really question how the fit would be (*PURE* honesty). Have you given that some thought? (Notice the "control questioning" technique at work; what interviewee Roger answers at this point may help enlighten your decision making...but minimally, it will let Roger know you're skeptical about this match).

(Continuing on now with **HUMILITY…**) Frankly, Roger, we really do need good help—in that regard, it's like we're always hiring. (And finally, a dose of **PATIENCE…**) I'm going to ask you to let me think about this, Roger, and I'll ask you to as well. I know you come very well referred by your cousin, Helen, and you seem like a great guy. I'm just such a firm believer in 'fit.' 'Like, making sure the round peg goes into the round hole."

You (**PHP** Manager) were honest on all counts, not cocky, and not rushing into any decisions. What happens after this: *cannot be written*. For the very next steps will be predicated on your inner sense kicking in. And it will, if you truly are **PURE, HUMBLE,** and **PATIENT,** fully APPRECIATING and ACCEPTING whatever happens. Make no mistake about it…it will be what's supposed to happen. Roger could either decide it's not the right job for him. Or when he tells his cousin (your present employee, Helen) "how he did," she may talk him out of it.

The thing is with **PHP**, you just don't know! That's the *inner sense* mechanism kicking in. Once you use it, and feel it working…you actually look forward to using it again. But it's always a pleasant surprise. For it's truly amazing.

"MIRRORING…" THE PHP MANAGER'S REPERTOIRE OF HONEST ROLES

Whenever we have a work situation where certain employees just don't seem to hit it off, we label it a personality conflict—or sometimes-bad chemistry. **PHP** research shows it's a lack of *mirroring*. Just as it sounds, when we mirror, reflect, imitate another, it feels and seems to that individual, like they're spending time with themselves. It's pleasant. People like people who are like them!

Here's an example of healthy, applied mirroring. You greet a new person at a large meeting. The first few words out of the person's mouth are softly spoken. That person will likely appreciate it, if you attempt to speak softly as well. Recall how loud, scary people often intimidate little kids—it does *not* reflect them. That's why we speak softly to babies. They tend to react more favorably.

They become happier. All adults are, are big kids. When you (**PHP** Manager) mirror employees to whom you're speaking, in groups or individually, they will naturally perceive you more comfortably. And in turn, whatever you're communicating to them, will be more readily accepted.

Here's an example of mirroring applied to interviewing. What's the main goal of an effective interview? In a word: honesty. A **PHP** Manager wants to gather the most *accurate* information in the shortest amount of interview time expended. Task one is to relax the situation. Sitting in a couple chairs around a table tends to informalize the format (as opposed to the almighty manager behind the huge, shiny, mahogany desk— remember ***HUMILITY***?). Beginning on time is a good idea; keeping people waiting tends to add more anxiety to an already stressful situation. When the interviewer is relaxed, communication will flow easier. Honesty takes a front seat. A mirroring clue for instance follows this sequence…a manager sits back and crosses his legs. Without even realizing, the interviewee crosses hers as well. In another case, an interviewing manager folds her hands. The interviewee folds his. Because the interviewee *likes* the manager, s/he will mirror that manager. In sequence, this interviewee is likely to be much more forthcoming, on why and why not—the job is a good match. Try this technique sometime. Sample it socially sometime even (AKA: "How to Get a Date"). You'll be amazed at the results.

SECTION B

Managing **Sticky Situations**
—Day-to-Day—

Chapter 5

Real *Motivating*

How to help employees get **unstuck**— *and watch them motorize and energize (and you too!)*

NOTES FROM THE PHP MANAGER'S JOURNAL...

"Motivate them? I can't even motivate me!"

> —OB, *Chicago*

"The people who are miserable will always be miserable."

> —DE, *Long Island*

"Our motto here is, 'It's always *opening day* for our customers. If it's not *opening day* for *you*, maybe someone else could work for you today. Tomorrow's a new day.'"

> —DENNIS DONOVAN, *Owner, Atlantic Seafood, Long Island*

37

STICKY NEWS

EXTRA, EXTRA, READ ALL ABOUT IT!

Anonymous Tip: *Employees Feel Unappreciated!*

Sources Say So Many Tasks Go Unrewarded—

NOT EVEN MENTIONED!

Pretend your employees have an underground grapevine newspaper. And pretend the above is today's headline. Do you:

A. Write an e-mail to all the employees stating how you *do* appreciate them?

B. Ignore it? (They're being paid).

C. Call a special meeting to clear the air?

D. Have an "Ice Cream Sundae Afternoon" to show them how much they're regarded?

E. Wait for performance review time and see if you can be a bit more generous with raises?

F. Form an "Employee Morale Committee?"

G. Ask a couple key, trusted employees if there's truth to the anonymous note?

H. Ask *your* boss what to do?

I. Write specific, hand-written thank-you notes to those employees you suspect may need some extra props?

Let's think out loud about potential next steps...

A. Some believe sending out a thank you e-mail is a cop-out to face-to-face vocalizing. Done sparingly however, and in combination with an ongoing MBWA (managing by wandering around) program, it's delicious, creamy icing on the cake.

B. Never ignore any discontent brought to your attention. Delay reaction perhaps…to think it all through—consider options. But never ignore. Managers are paid for the quality of their thinking, from which stems high caliber decisions.

C. Meetings-schmeetings. There's better stuff to do first. See Chapter Eight…*(Non-*Sticky*) Teamwork* and Organizing *Great Meetings,* How to inspire groups to just plain, work better, together!

D. Best time to buy donuts, pizza, whatever is 1) When you *don't* feel the need to *buy* accolades from your employees; 2) When they *don't* expect it. Expected perks become "hygiene factors." More on this later.

E. Generally, *nothing* should wait 'til evaluation time. No surprises. And money can't buy you love or (sustained) employee loyalty. Sure, they'll fake it for awhile but feigned love and loyalty of any kind is as empty as a beer bottle tossed into a field in the hazy drought of summer.

F. "Employee Morale Committee?" See "C." See "D." IOW, it's not the first "what to do now."

G. You may acquire the info you need, but putting "pet" employees on the spot makes them feel like snitches. **PHP** Managers don't need informants. They're *out there* recognizing the problems before they exist.

H. One question: does your boss use **PHP**? If so, ask away. If not, don't.

I. "Thank you" notes? See "D."

So what's the answer? Let's first discuss what often does *not* work. We in traditional supervision confuse activity with effectiveness. IOW, we think we need to act—to do something! We conventionally-trained managers like to have answers for everything!

ACTION BRIEF! *It's okay to answer employees' questions with "That's a good question…I'm not sure?"*

Here's an idea for a possible solution. Take a walk. Stroll around. If you're employees are not used to it, they may freak a bit, but just do it. Greet them. Sincerely ask them how things are going. Just chat. No agendas. No known purpose. You're serving them. An old <u>In Search of Excellence</u> adage was that if you're not serving the customer (internal or external), then you should be serving someone who is. We managers are not on the revenue side of the income statement. We're expenses. If/when they ask you *what's up* or if you *need anything*, simply say "No, just checking in," or whatever's natural for you to say (***PURITY, HUMILITY***). Don't expect to discover any ah-hahs (***PATIENCE***). And when you go back to your office, and think to yourself what a friggin' waste of time that was, know this: you have no idea the potential, positive impact you made. And you may never know—for this is part of the perpetual building of a motivational workplace environment. This is MBWA (managing by wandering around). You never motivate employees; your best hope is to create an atmosphere where *maybe* employees can motivate themselves.

This philosophy can and should become your MO. The more routine it becomes the more familiar and comfortable will be your presence. Your approachability increases exponentially. As this transpires, you become safer as a person with whom to informally chat. Now you can request ideas and methods to improve their jobs. Productivity and ultimately company profit will follow. Something like this: "Hey guys! Here's where we are numbers-wise, here's where we want to be (***PURITY***).

We in management feel we have a pretty good direction, but we're not certain about the best way to execute the strategy (*HUMILITY*)... specifically with the day-to-day stuff you all do. Will you all please think about some ways to basically improve the workflow here? Policies, procedures, your particular tasks...everything. Nothing's too small or too big to consider." Now depending on the level of comfort and trust the employees have in your sincerity, will be the amount of output delivered. But give it time (*PATIENCE*). Trust is a big, powerful steam roller. When it finally starts, it builds momentum—slowly, then faster. Never speedy, but always strong.

Crucial **PHP** Reaction Tip: *If* you're fortunate enough to glean feedback from your employees, it may not always be music to your ears. Being human, you may hastily become defensive—briskly rationalizing why it wouldn't work. Instead, shut up (*PATIENCE*); if you ever want them to share their thoughts again. There's always time after it seeps in and percolates a bit (*HUMILITY*) to get back to them with feedback on their suggestions (*PATIENCE*).

THE CHICKEN OR THE EGG?

Which comes first: morale or productivity? Do you try to make employees happy and they work hard? Or do you help them be productive (busy, prolific, profitable) and hope they inherit happiness in the process? The jury's been out on this one forever. There's a little known tale of the New York Yankees of yesteryear (the era of pennant after pennant). Allegedly, some of the guys didn't like some of the other guys very much. You could say they had some employee morale issues. But when they were pouring champagne all over each other in the locker rooms...the "personality problems" seemed to warrant no discussion.

So just for kicks, let's say the egg comes first. This would be *productivity* if you're staying up with the story. Simply put, employees should be held accountable for the quality and quantity of "eggs" they make, ship, sell, etc. Chickens are. As was discussed in Chapter Three, hard, accurate, *productivity* number results tell a mammoth part of the story. Oh sure, there's certain conditions you as the chicken manager can create—proper temperature in the coop, clean nest boxes, enriched food. Yes, employees are animals, but possess refinements our poultry brethren do not.

"Hygiene Factors" as described by Frederick Herzberg have nothing to do with *being clean.* They are instead the things we expect at work—break time to eat during a work shift, access to a rest room when needed, getting paid. A "Motivating Factor" in Herzberg's "Two-Factor Theory" would be an unexpected raise, or being given an opportunity to advance at work. When *motivators* become *hygiene*, they lose their humph. Remember Chevy Chase in <u>Christmas Vacation</u>? He bought a swimming pool with a Christmas bonus he *expected* to get; but his boss had other plans—namely the "jelly of the month club." Or as his cousin, Eddie said, "The gift that keeps on giving!" Chevy's character treated the bonus as a hygiene factor. No happy surprise, and with little appreciation—it lost its motivating ability. You'll learn in Chapter Seven, there should be no surprises with employees, especially at review time. Let's add a corollary: *under-promise but over-deliver.* IOW, good surprises are good!

Instead of buying pastries every Thursday morning, switch it up. Skip a week. Then the next, serve bagels with veggie cream cheese. **PHP** Managers find their employees are motivated by *not knowing* what their raises will be each year. If/when the productivity is properly measured, and compensation awarded accordingly, employees really are in charge of their destinies—short term leading to long. They will perpetually be self-measuring: *what's in it for me?!* And the loop is splendidly closed when they are able to answer the question for themselves as well. Keep them on their toes (like a small guy at a urinal). BTW, this *good surprise* stuff is applicable in marriage, raising kids, teaching students, and serving customers. Think about it. We all like presents!

THIMK! *If employees are "on," they rarely have to be managed. And the days of them jumping into action just when they see you will be long gone. It should get to a point where you can almost feel like you're not even earning your money.*

MEASURE WHAT'S IMPORTANT

What you reward tends to get repeated explains Michael LeBoeuf in describing what he states is the *greatest management principle in the world.* (From the book with the same title from 1985). He calls it GMP. Back to the chicken coop for a moment, if the hens don't care whether you put the food in one big bowl, or numerous small bowls, and egg quality and quantity are unaffected…then the chicken manager shouldn't care either. Point is, many of us over-concentrate on minor crap—which is all it is. **PHP** Managers prioritize those chores and duties which influence *results.* Interestingly, this powerful stuff works when managing and directing volunteer groups as well. Pattye Pece, President of Sobornost for The World Foundation, believes that "Management works best when you delegate what needs to be delegated and then step back and allow them to do their jobs." Pece continues, "Ask your employees or volunteers to give you ideas that will help your business or foundation grow and then include them in the plans."

ACTION BRIEF! Get out of their way. Front-line employees almost always know better than the supervisor.

TWO BUMS WALK INTO A TRAIN STATION…

No joke. They really did! And there was one other guy in there (suit-type with fancy briefcase, nice coat, etc.). It was a snowy-icy-cold morning, no heat or even lights nor any ticket-selling attendant. It was the "suit" and the two bums. All of a sudden, a chill pervaded the spine of the "suit," as the bums were just standing behind him. He smelled a working cigarette and detected the stomach-turning aroma of stale wine from the night before. The "suit" considered that these guys could pretty much kill him and nobody would know for hours. He thought about striking up a conversation with them, "Hey, homeless guys, how's it going?" But he would never use that description—besides, could they even talk? The 6:07AM train for which the "suit" was waiting was awfully late, so he checked the schedule. It was actually the 7:06. Oh no! His anxiousness heightened to fright. And then, astonishingly, they spoke! Here's part of their conversation:

Pete: "You goin' to the turkey dinner tonight at 4:00?"

JC: "For the homeless?"

Pete: "Yeah. You goin'?"

JC: "Yes, uh, huh. Went last year. Was pretty good."

Pete: (After a couple minutes) "Slept at Dunkin' donuts last night."

JC: "Least it's warm."

Pete: "That's the main thing."

The whole thrust of Maslow's Hierarchy is about appreciating what we have—in levels...in degrees. Placed in another perspective, do you or I really think about where our next meal is coming from? Or heaven help us, where we'll sleep tonight?! The homeless guys may or may not have known those answers. And you would think they'd be on the first level of Maslow's Hierarchy (physiological needs: food, clothing, shelter). But maybe, just maybe they were closer to the top (highest level is "self-actualization," like they've reached it...had it all). They didn't seem concerned...about anything.

What are *you* concerned about? Would people be surprised if they knew? One more time, *would people be surprised if they knew what concerned you?!* The answer is yes. The moral in this (true) fable: we have very little idea what those guys in the train station were thinking and feeling. And just as true is that we cannot "size up" our employees' thoughts, feelings, desires, and aspirations. No one *ever* motivates another. It's always an inside job.

"MOTIVATE THIS!"

So how do you motivate…you? DON'T depend on your boss for this—ever. All the things you do for your employees—planning, measuring, feedback…you must do for yourself as well. Pay attention to what you want to *repeat* in your life. Your reward will be the tremendous intrinsic feeling that you're *on!* On purpose. On schedule. On course. On fire, baby! The more regularly you summon **PURITY, HUMILITY** and **PATIENCE**, the more your *inner sense* will reward your actions. This in turn, increases your self-confidence. You'll stride with passion. You'll do what you say you will—and this charismatic reputation will precede you and follow you.

Chapter 6

Smooth
Delegating

How to give out jobs...and actually have them get done!

NOTES FROM THE PHP MANAGER'S JOURNAL...

"You don't want to ask your employees to do jobs? Sure, it'd be nice if they just saw what had to be done—*and did it.* But maybe that's why we need managers in the first place?"

—**VICE-PRESIDENT** *(high-tech manufacturing corporation in NY); her span of control is approximately 45 employees.*

STICKY NEWS

EXTRA, EXTRA, READ ALL ABOUT IT!

Overheard Phone Conversation: "No, I can still talk...that's just my manager telling me to do something..."

You're a newly-minted, young supervisor...and to complicate it even further, you used to work with some of the employees you're now managing. You overheard one of your employees utter the above statement on a personal call on the phone at work. Do you:

A. Stick your little finger on their phone, ending the call? (No one talks like that on your watch!)

B. Just disregard the comment, pretending not to have heard it?

C. Do the task yourself, insuring its completion?

D. Admit to them you're embarrassed and a scaredy-cat—to ask them to do anything?

E. Tell them you need to meet with them tomorrow at 4:00 PM, and just let them dwell on the unknown topic?

F. Go stand in front of them while they're on the phone?

G. Grab the phone out of their hand, and converse with the other party, asking, "Did she just say she could still talk, that was just my manager?!"

H. Write her a note with the task on it, with what was to be done, and by when?

I. Ask her why she said that?

So what's the prob here? Basically, we're not being taken seriously. For some reason perhaps this employee doesn't feel a sense of accountability.

In other words, if they don't do it (whatever the task is), what's the worst that can happen? Let's look at some potential reactions to the letter choices.

A. Tough guy. Dramatic. Yeah, you'll hush the crowds, but they'll think you're a horse's rear-end. And you are. Treat them like kids, and they'll act like kids—to each other and your clients/customers. You've given them a license to do it.

ACTION BRIEF! Don't even treat <u>kids</u> like kids (see above paragraph for reason).

B. Pretend it didn't happen? Maybe a good option. At least you're not giving it energy. Still doesn't completely fix the problem though; will have to be complemented with another strategy.

C. "If you want something done, do it yourself." Unfortunately, this has become the mantra of waaaay too many managers, struggling to get it all done in a day; and frequent complaining becomes just a part of life.

D. Admit you're a whimp? Sure does satisfy the **HUMILITY** gig, huh? Probably shouldn't use it as a stand-alone though. Better to blend it in with another strategy (use a Black and Tan Beer visual if it makes you happy).

E. Keep 'em in suspense? Foolish use of your power. The time they spend worrying in uncertainty will be time they're not producing for you.

F. Be an impolite nuisance hovering over them? Again, you're wasting good, potential power. Would you like someone doing that to you?

G. Does this even deserve an answer?

H. This one deserves some thought. Less oral interaction needed (not necessarily a bad thing), and the clear written word is difficult to challenge. It's a pictorial way of inquiring: why wasn't it done? More on this later in the chapter.

I. Ask why? We learned that the person (**PHP** Manager) asking questions is in control of the situation. We almost don't have to ever say anything—IF we're asking the right, simple questions in a non-emotional/"pass the butter" sort of way.

Try this sample dialogue on for size. (Note: this conversation took place just after the incident occurred…m-a-y-b-e that wasn't the best idea for starters?!) (Setting: manager's office, clear desk, employee's chair three feet back from the front of the manager's desk).

MANAGER: "Valerie, I need to talk to you about getting things done around here." (Employee a bit surprised by the tone).

VALERIE: "O-kaaay…"

MANAGER: (Tapping gold pen on polished desk) "You know, we actually don't need as many employees as we currently have on board. This ship's getting a lit-tle heavier than it needs to be. (Valerie's silent, not sure what to do or say). And even IF people are kept on board, well we certainly don't have to keep giving everyone full-time hours. Times are tough out there you know!"

VALERIE: "But I thought the company was doing pretty good latel—"

MANAGER: (Interrupts) "Oh the company is doing okay. It's certain employees that are going to find themselves with their hours all dried up. I personally could jump in and take the place of at least two of you."

Doesn't this manager sound like a delight with whom to work? Imagine what a blast they are at home? We're not talking life of the party material here. Yet even if you, yes you—think you'd never talk that way, parts of the message often creep through like water seeping through basement walls. Quiet, but damaging.

Threatening schedule decreases, even if a realistic possibility is as much a pain for the manager. S/he'd do better with, "We need you here, Valerie. If you weren't here, I'd have to do your work until I hired the right people—and you well know that's no easy task." It's probably truer (**PURITY**). It's letting them into the inner sanctum of your problem world (**HUMILITY**). **PATIENCE** in this case would be asking them to help you. You may even want to admit you have trouble just accomplishing your own job. It really is okay to let them see you sweat a little, contrary to what the debate coach told you.

End game, you (**PHP** Manager) are the clean-up batter; doing what you gotta' do. APPRECIATE what they *do* do for you, and ACCEPT with **PATIENCE** what they don't.

IF YOU DELEGATE PROPERLY, YOU'LL BE HAPPY WITH YOUR FEET ON YOUR DESK BY ELEVEN IN THE MORNING

Ridiculous though it sounds, this *is* the ultimate litmus test of effective delegation. *Can the joint function without you around?* But an even better question is (brace yourselves with a big, fat dose of **HUMILITY**): can the joint function *better* without you around?!

"Theory X" leadership, introduced by Douglas McGregor, says essentially that you should be around, that employees are basically lazy—and if you turn your back on them, they'll screw you whenever the opportunity arises. Sometimes, this is similar to what is referred to as "autocratic" managing, contrasted to a more democratic type of leading people. This is closer to what McGregor called "Theory Y." This practice utilizes more MBO (managing by objectives) where everyone knows the objective, the goal; how it gets managed will be determined by the group.

This philosophy also encourages "emergent" leadership. Natural leaders (if they exist) seem to pop out and flower, and can be most beneficial to an organization. They sort of make themselves responsible for tasks. This soft, often unwritten, self-empowerment earns them the respect and likability of others—both bosses and other employees. Eventually, they are often given the official authority to carry out tasks.

(Note: **PHP** Managers are diligent for sustaining *happy mediums*. Sometimes, "overly-emergent" employees *kick-butt and ask questions later*. This can create more problems than it solves. It's all part of our positions as perpetual trainers and developers of our people. As Jack says on <u>Without a Trace</u>, "It's my job. It's what I do." Training, developing, and nurturing our people *is our job)*.

The material discussed in the last couple paragraphs can frequently go strategically awry if the manager doesn't focus and pay close intuitive attention. Generally it is risky to give an employee the responsibility to carry out a task without the authority to complete it. A quickie example of this is leaving an employee "in charge" but failing to advise the rest of the group: who's boss. Surprisingly, it happens all too often.

Let's go back to Option H earlier in this chapter, as promised. This was providing (mainly) written instructions for employees. Then afterwards, we can simply ask them *why* task(s) were not completed/accomplished. As you recall, questions are effective. The person asking questions is in control of the situation. You, **PHP** Manager will deal with whatever answers pop up with something called situational leadership. In other words, you'll only know what to say *after* you've heard the response(s) from the employee.

Backspace to Option H…*write her a note with the task on it, what exactly has to be done, and by when?* A hybrid example of this is a manager who has three employees. She leaves a list for all three to accomplish on her day off. Next day results? Almost *nothing* done on the list. Because individual productivity could *not* be tracked (like seeing who rang which sales, for instance; i.e. Big-Mouth-Millie in Chapter Three), the manager asked the group. Still, no clear answers…"It was just busy, not really sure where the time went," and the like. The **PHP** Manager in this case realized that a separate list for each individual was the way to go. Though it discouraged teamwork, it encouraged greater accountability. Some "teams" need this more than others.

Okay, so would it be weird to be catching some mid-morning Zs in your office—feet up and all? Yeah, I'm sure your boss would appreciate stopping in and seeing that too, huh?! C'mon, admit it. You couldn't even deal with the guilt you'd feel, could ya'?! But that's the real goal of delegation…for you, the **PHP** Manager to be able to sit and think.

THIMK! *Thinking is hard work. You're paid to think; new procedures, new marketing ideas, new programs.*

Unfortunately, there is a serious lack of thinking today—evident in our schools, companies, even homes. **PHP** Managers become confident with just…thinking. Thinking is hard work. It is said that Andrew Carnegie payed Charles Schwab $75,000 for what he did; and another million for what he got others to do. Think about that!

Sure there are lots of reasons *not* to delegate. Empower employees (buzz phrase from a decade or so ago) too much, and chaos occurs. But remember when you won that trip to Belize, and it was your first vacation in two years? You thought, "What's the worst thing that could happen?" in your absence. You didn't dwell on it, but just told yourself, "Okay, I could even deal with that *worst*…so I'm going." Business COOs often refer to this as the *critical path*. And then simply prepare, plan, and organize to try to prevent it, by forging a smooth flow of workplace activity—*in your absence!*

Let go, my friend…or you'll be doing it all yourself (at work and at home). Less trying on your part. More trusting on your part. Use **PHP**, and then trust that under-rated inner sense. Can't lose.

PROPERLY <u>DELEGATING</u>
SHOULD FEEL LIKE…

A Hundred and One Things that Feel Good!

 # 28: "*Seems like your longest day in history. Two- hour flight with your new boss at five AM. She kicks off her shoes on the plane, but you realize you have a hole in your sock. Meetings at nine, eleven, and*

three. You break at about six to check into your hotel room; meeting back in the lobby at seven for dinner. Half past six now—you melt into that cushy chair in your private room and thrust off your shoes, kicking them clear across the room. Your dogs have never been so happy!" (Sensory bonus: you close your eyes and olfactoraly recall your childhood—entering hotel/motel rooms with your family. You never knew what that pleasant, clean smell was—still don't; but it still give your nose warm fuzzies).

Chapter 7

Teflon Appraising for *Effective Performance* Evaluation

How to better use this valuable tool...

with or without raises!

NOTES FROM THE PHP MANAGER'S JOURNAL...

"Whether catching someone in a lie or telling a friend she has bad breath, these are real issues that make us simultaneously uncomfortable, frustrated, and disappointed. Learning to be patient with, accept, and even appreciate others' foibles while recognizing

55

their strengths is not easy, but it's certainly valuable advice. The outcome can only be an improvement in your ability to work productively with others."

—**DR. MANNY LONDON**, *Faculty Director Undergraduate College of Leadership & Service State University of New York, Stony Brook, NY*

STICKY NEWS
EXTRA, EXTRA, READ ALL ABOUT IT!

It's Almost Review Time, But Jenny Smells... Real Bad!

"I'd rather have double root canal, than have to tell an employee s/he has a personal odor problem!"

—**ANON.**

Jenny is a great worker. She also smells. Do you...

A. Write her a memo, suggesting that she see a physician? For often, it's a minor medical problem.

B. Ask a close co-worker to subtly bring it to her attention? She'll be far less embarrassed that way.

C. Just wait it out? These things always have a way of working themselves out.

D. Leave deodorant in her drawer? She'll get the hint, and will be even less embarrassed than in "B" (above).

E. Just wait for the review?

F. Use **PHP**? And go from there.

Ah yes, the age-old problem of an offensive employee. 'Doesn't get much **stickier** than that, huh?! How do managers handle the problem? They *don't* handle it, that's how! Call it wishful thinking maybe…but for some reason, managers hope that by avoiding the situation, it will go away. It does not. It MUST be addressed. And don't wait for review time. There should never be surprises on a performance evaluation. The review meeting should include lots of phrases like "…as we discussed." The process is ongoing.

First, here's how not to deal with any type of personal odor. You'll notice it didn't say "hygiene" problem. Your (**Sticky** People Problem-Solving Manager) main concern is not the *root* problem at this point, contrary to what you may have been advised. Your job is to deal with the symptoms affecting the workplace flow. In fact, the problem itself may actually be none of your business. Your job is to correct the situation, so it no longer, ugh-ugh…distracts customers and other employees. "Stop the stink" is your mission here.

So back to how *not* to deal with it? Many managers and even fellow employees think the best way to address the situation is by subtle hints… leaving cans of deodorant and soap lying around. These actions, though paved with good intentions, are potential law suit material; causing stress, confusion, and bad feelings.

When reading the following scenario, see if you can pick out what a mediocre manager might say, and which might be the words of a **PHP** Manager.

> **JENNY** (Employee): "Hey boss, you wanted to see me? I can't talk for too long, my husband's in the car with the kids. I have (Jenny looks at her watch) almost five o'clock, is that right?"

> **MANAGER:** "Yeah, I won't keep you too long. I just wanted to say…"

> **JENNY:** (Interrupting with excitement) "Hey, why not walk me out to the car, and see your new little Godson?! Thanks for saying *yes!* We're honored to have such a wonderful Godfather!"

MANAGER: "Yeah, ah, actually, Jen, I ah...have to tell you something. It's kind of a tricky thing to..."

JENNY: "Boss, I got your back, whatever it is. I'm there for you! Talk to me."

MANAGER: "Jenny, I uhm, well I'm not sure how to...Jenny, you're a great person—and the last thing I want to do is..."

EMPLOYEE: (Interrupting) "Are you firing me, boss?"

MANAGER: "No, it's just that...well, the way you sometimes come off to people is..."

JENNY: "Is Jimbo complaining about me again, boss? I'll talk to him. It's just that the rest of us work so damn hard, and this guy's milkin' it! So I bust his chops a bit."

MANAGER: (Quietly interrupting) "It's sort of an odor problem, Jenny."

JENNY: "Oh yeah, he does get ripe sometimes! Jimbo's not a bad guy..."

MANAGER: (Quickly, more loudly interrupting) "It's not Jimbo, Jen. (Pause). It's you. (Pause). I'm sorry to..."

JENNY: (Rises abruptly and begins walking out) "I gotta' go, boss. The kids are waiting."

MANAGER: "But Jen, ah..." (Jenny's gone).

Now what?! How does the manager feel? Did he (in this case) succeed in the conversation? How does Jenny feel? Will the main problem be permanently corrected now? Even if it is, what damage was done to the manager/employee relationship?

Most of the answers to these questions unfortunately lead towards the negative column. The answers are not very happy. And the fact is, there are even **more** unanswered ones. Jenny still doesn't know the depth of the problem. She's missing some vital details. And the manager is thinking: did he blow it?

Which he did, by the way.

Let's rewind a bit. Why do managers choose the end of the day (and in particular on Fridays), to address tough problems like this one—and firing people as well? They do it so they can "leave" the whole situation for a spell (like an entire weekend); so they're not reminded of that uncomfortable feeling.

Yet, here's what makes Jenny's situation even worse: who, now, does Jenny take it out on? Her husband and kids. This is not healthy, contrary to what some may think. Anything coming from Jenny now will be purely emotional. All her husband can do here is just be brought down too.

If she were still at work, however, she may or may not "unload" with personal negative feedback. But instead, Jenny would just chill a bit, so that she could focus on herself; and just think. She would think how she doesn't feel like she has control over the present state of affairs. But mostly, Jenny would be embarrassed. She'd think about how her boss mishandled the situation. And how what, if anything, she could have done to fix this predicament.

Now, let's look at a better way to handle this challenge. A **PHP** Manager would first choose a time and place where Jenny could remain for a while after the conversation—for as long as she needed. An effective dialogue might go something like this.

> **MANAGER:** "Jenny, I want to bring something to your attention. It's been shared with me, out of concern, that you have a personal odor problem. Please don't ask me how, or from where it came to my attention, because that's not the issue. I DO want you to know that 'everybody is NOT talking about it.' I wanted to talk to you myself before it got out of hand." (Notice the ***PURITY).***

> (**MANAGER** continues) "I'm sure this is uncomfortable to hear, and frankly, I feel a bit funny talking about it myself. But if I were in your shoes, I certainly would want someone to make me aware. That's really all I have to say, Jenny. It'll stay

between us. I've found that in the past, just making someone aware of a concern was enough to fix the problem." (Catch the **HUMILITY,** shared with a dose of **PATIENCE).** "I jotted down notes of this conversation, just because we document almost everything around here. You can initial just to acknowledge that we talked, or choose not to. You can even have a copy if you like. It'll just go into a very private file from here."

Jenny could become very ticked-off at you, raise her voice...or cry— or just leave. Now you, **PHP** Manager, must know that however this conversation ends, you have done your job. This is a key point. Don't look for positive feedback from the employee on the way you handled the situation. In other words, don't be waiting for Jenny to come back to you and say, "Hey boss, I just wanted to say thank you again, for handling that situation so well with me before. What you said made perfect sense, and I'm really going to try to do it. 'You know what else, boss? You're a really awesome manager, and I love working for you!"

Don't hold your breath! It ain't gonna' happen! **PHP** Managers simply have to believe, and know, s/he is doing the right thing. Any feedback that ***does*** in fact come back to you—is a very nice bonus. Just don't count on it. Just know that you have done the right thing.

ACTION BRIEF! *Always do the right thing, even when those above you and below you, may not.*

THIMK! **PHP** *Manager Idea Tip: Note that in over 85 percent of cases, the simple act of merely making the employee "aware," will be enough to fix the problem. A lot of times, managers like to throw in that "...it could be a medical problem." But* **PHP** *Managers know that's only a (hopeful) scapegoat. Less than seven percent of cases are due to true medical problems.*

Using the phrasing above is humane, kind, and effective. You'll be amazed at the results. 'Worst possible case: it doesn't work. Now further discussion or even disciplinary action has to occur (See Chapter Ten, ***Disciplining and Firing—'almost always* sticky,** How to do it (when you have to): <u>safely</u> and <u>calmly</u> while staying out of court! But keep thinking positively, and you'll likely avoid that step.

Two more items of note in the aforementioned **PHP** conversation… you'll notice that the manager made no small talk at the beginning, even though there was probably time to do it (it ***wasn't*** the end of the day). The less "distraction," the better—cut to the chase. 'Secondly, being the Godfather to an employee's kid is a nice thing, yet a large, ongoing challenge of effective managing is staying aware, of just how much distance to keep. It's a perpetual process. **PHP** Managers are cognitive of how involved or uninvolved to get, in the lives of their employees.

Wouldn't you like to be totally open and honest with your employees, never having to look over your shoulder? There's a particular mind-easiness that evolves with ***full disclosure.*** A clear conscience is the highest octane available.

PHP…***PURITY, HUMILITY, PATIENCE.*** Trust your inner sense. It never fails. It's always effective.

CASH IS KING—"JUST PUT IT IN OUR PAYCHECKS…MAYBE NOT."

Many surveys reflect that when managers are asked—what employees place at the top of the list, they believe their employees will say salary, money, cold cash! When employees are posed the same question, however, "Good wages" comes up about number four out of ten. The number one spot? "Interesting work" is the winner. Employees want to engage, not just pass time.

They desire not to look busy, but to be busy. It's a human, inherent condition to serve a need, to make a contribution.

Think about it. Could most of your employees (maybe even you!) leave their jobs today, and get a higher-paying position in a couple weeks? The answer is a resounding: yes. I didn't say better hours, or convenient proximity, or nicer co-workers. The question was simply more money. Yet they ***don't*** leave because of the reasons just alluded to.

Knowing this, **PHP** Managers appraise employees regularly and continually. The concept of MBWA was introduced in *the* business book of the last century, <u>In Search of Excellence</u>. It stands for "managing by walking around," or "wandering about." MBWA means to get out into the stockrooms, the sales floors, the factories, the farm fields...wherever the employees are.

Sam Walton used to ask his rank and file store associates two questions, "What do you need?" and "What's selling?" Oh sure, he could have gathered data in a more efficient manner—but felt a need to personally connect. As the story goes, old Sam used to occasionally hitch a ride on his delivery trucks. If you want to know what's going on, what better market research than to ask the driver who travels store-to-store?! Ask your employees sincerely, how they are doing. Is there anything you can do for them? This helps **PHP** Managers remain approachable. And being easy to talk to—is the first step towards using regular (almost daily) performance appraisal. When you do have to discipline an employee on an issue, often it can be in normal conversation. (HR Note: of course you'll need to follow your company's policies and procedures for documenting meetings; or at least be consistent with how conversations are held). **PHP** Managers appraise in short blips, and appraise frequently. This system is far superior to waiting until the annual review, and then blurting out multiple surprises.

A common (poor) managerial technique is to write the annual review (full of shockers which should have been at least mentioned during the year), and leave it in a sealed envelope at the end of the day. The less-than-competent manager is nowhere to be found—intentionally, when the POed employee tries tracking him down. The manager's already on her second "cold one" at home, praying that the overnight calms the irate nerves of the employee. Which actually will happen. But the long-term consequence will be far greater communication barriers—resulting in even less approachability.

There should be NO surprises on reviews (written and/or oral)! This includes pay raises and bonuses. In some companies, employees spend their end-of-the-year bonuses in July! Just like Chevy Chase did it in

<u>Christmas Vacation</u>. He pre-purchased a built-in swimming pool. Your employees will really be okay with "no raises this year." Explain **why.** (**PHP** is absolutely infused in this word). If the economy stinks, but they like working with you, don't be surprised if they "jump on board…" support you—***take your back!***

Another scenario: employee wants more money, but doesn't deserve it? This can definitely get **sticky**. Especially when a particular job has few objective measures—like sales in dollars, accounts opened, calls made successfully, sandwiches made, and so on. Try this phrasing on for size.

"Aiden, I wanted to chat with you for a bit concerning your request for a raise. I appreciate your bringing it to my attention, because it's important for me to know what people are thinking (***PURITY***—honest APPRECIATION). I gave your request careful thought, Aiden, cause frankly…I was uncertain what to do (***HUMILITY***—ACCEPTING the fact you ***don't*** have all the answers). You do an adequate job now, not superior—not deserving of a raise in my managerial opinion. But I'm ***not*** going to say 'no.' Instead, we're going to try something for eight weeks. Here are some suggestions for you, Aiden; some things to try over the next couple of months." (At this juncture, the **PHP** Manager gives specific, hopefully measurable tasks for the employee to achieve).

The **PHP** Manager (assuming s/he has the authority to do this) should then give the range of what the/a merit raise might be—no promises, of course. Remember the wonderfully-wise expression to "under-promise and over-deliver." That's what **PHP** Managers do. If the range shared with Aiden is .8 to 1.6 percent, you should know he'll be looking for the higher number. In fact, he won't be able to shake it from his mind. Over delivering in this case, might be a 1.75 percent increase, and 2 percent will put 'em over the positive, motivational edge!

Now, what's vital during this period is regular, frequent evaluation of the situation. Informality is fine. MBWA is integral. You'll know pretty quickly if he's improving. Keep him apprised…help him to ***improve his performance***. And if he doesn't, there's lots of "Plan Bs." But that'll depend on how where your **PHP** inner sense takes you. Aiden might realize himself: he doesn't deserve more money, but will have a new appreciation for your management communication techniques. Or he may leave. But keep thinking positively. It's the **PHP** way.

The environment nurtured by this type of **PHP** Management creates a self-perpetuating flow of employees *assessing themselves*. You, by your regular evaluations, assistance, instructions…teach them how. Employees become their own best coaches! As supervisors use more and more **PHP** techniques, they feel an increasing sense of control. Good control. Positive command.

Chapter 8

(*Non*-Sticky) Teamwork and Organizing Great Meetings

How to inspire groups to just plain,
work better, together!

NOTES FROM THE PHP MANAGER'S JOURNAL...

"Sure, we have a policy on meetings in our company. There are none, ever. No further discussion."

—FICTITIOUS CEO, *Fictitious Fortune 100 Company*

S T I C K Y   N E W S

EXTRA, EXTRA, READ ALL ABOUT IT!

Pretend Middle Manager Slides Through Another Work Day!

THREE LONG MEETINGS SCHEDULED YIELD NO TIME FOR REAL WORK, AND LOTS OF AMMO FOR EXCUSES

Tom Peters said managers who push paper from one side of the desk to the other are assholes. This chapter begins with some radical quotes and headlines because *teams and team meetings* run improperly are responsible for much of the demise of American productivity. You may recall the use of the words *accountability, responsibility,* and *authority* from Chapter Two. Proper teamwork tactics are potent fertilizer for unaccountability, shirking responsibility, and confusing who's in charge of what—resulting in status quo finger-pointing and scapegoating. So what's a middle (or any level) PHP Manager to do? *Emerge* will be our word of choice for this chapter.

First, an illustration to stress just a bit more—how silently, subtly dangerous this concept can be if misused. Remember your first year college Sociology class? The professor luuuved putting the class in groups. There was the one kid who always took over—pointing, directing and counting to make sure there were exactly six students. Sounds okay, as we need *emergent* leaders; but this kid was a rear-end-kissing, know-it-all (the kind of person that makes you glad when s/he can't make the company summer barbeque). This kid ran the group in class. He made all the decisions. The exercises entailed little teamwork *except* when s/he fingered the blame to another member for anything the teacher questioned. Fun, huh?! You know this cat—there's one in every classroom and workplace.

Then there's the other kid. You remember him: hat and hoody covering as much of his face as humanly possible. The pages of his books (when he bothered to bring them) never saw the light of day. Never had a pen.

And when it came time to move into groups, he'd hesitate; maybe glance at the clock on the wall…wondering why he even got up this morning, much less enrolled in this college. Finally caving into professor-pestering, he would acquiesce by sliding his chair into the group circle. But not really in it, just off to the side enough to subtly state his disinterest in being part of this team. You know this cat today too. S/he's either the miserable loner three cubicles down from you, or the upbeat, wealthy entrepreneur or intrapreneur (three cubicles down from you).

SO HOW DO YOU REALLY INSPIRE GROUPS TO JUST WORK BETTER, TOGETHER?

All we are as working adults are big kids. So to answer the above question, let's turn back the clocks to fifth grade (man, you were cute!). Recall the ten-year-old boys playing that game where one falls back and the others catch him. They think it's funny to let their buddy fall once in a while. Still and all, young men and young women really do trust each other—in the important things of life. Thirty years later, when the highly-paid management consultant comes in to conduct team building, guess what game they play? "Fall back!" But this time the (big) boys *always* catch each other. Does this mean they trust each other more now than when they were in fifth grade? (Think about that question). Funny thing about trust: it takes a perpetual lifetime to build…and can be lost in a flash.

THIMK! *Outcomes and people will be mediocre when trust is absent from the climate. If you trust yourself first, then you will trust others. Then they will trust you. It's a wonderful cycle.*

Fifth-graders band because they *want to*. The reciprocity is simple and honest (***PURE***). They hang together to play ball, video games, or share their common avocation in scaring their sisters with fake spiders. That age bracket hosts very little in the way of hidden agendas. They *want* to be "team-mates." They have emerged as team members. Sure, they exchange pushes once in a while—but it's minus secret back-biting and covert sabotaging. But then we grow up. "Maturity" is rather oxymoronic however (on the ball field for example). For when the coaches formalize structure, and egotistical parents over-stick-in their two cents, it sometimes gets downright stupid. Yes, we sometimes do seem to go backwards in life.

PHP Managers allow teams to form naturally, whether it's to accomplish a particular task in the short-run, or a longer-term strategic goal. Sometimes this is referred to as *organizational development.* A good "OD" program says that one plus one does not equal two. Instead, the sum is three, five, and seven in some cases! Synergy. It occurs when something becomes more effective working together, than it ever could with people working separately. It happens on the playground and can happen at work too. People (of all ages) are enjoying themselves; into their tasks…heart and soul. AKA, making your own good time.

Encouraging your employees to emerge, and aptly using MBO, results in employees deciding their own outcomes *and how to get there.* They will naturally think harder, smarter, and clearer about it.

ACTION BRIEF! *Be a good team member: on the field, at home, and in the office. Your employees will model you.*

SO WHAT DOES ALL THIS HAVE TO DO WITH MEETINGS?

When you have effective teams, the next step is to sanction them to plan and hold their own meetings. A skeptical rebuke is, "Yeah right, social hour." The key is to hold your employees responsible for work results. Not time, and not loyalty based on "Well, they're always there." Sure, that holds some weight. But when you're looking at objective fact and figure *results,* you'll be amazed how few meetings they'll call. *They'll* be holding themselves accountable. Sounds too easy? Hopefully by this chapter, it's becoming clear that solid people managing is not hard. Done right, PHP makes solving sticky people problems smooth as shadow mountain wine.

Chapter 9

Resolving Sticky Conflicts

*How to get up the courage to handle
scary employee situations!*

NOTES FROM THE PHP MANAGER'S JOURNAL...

"A good manager must check his or her ego at the front door, give credit to employees when things go well, and take responsibility when they do not."

—**JUDY YOUNG,** *(former) VP, Special Projects, Abilities, Inc.,
Albertson, NY*

"Dealing with conflict reminds me of the occasional noise I hear in my car. I tell myself it will go away. Not only does it not go away but it also brings a hefty repair bill with it because I have ignored the problem. When dealing with conflict, you must not run away from it or say it doesn't exist. Be courageous and deal with conflict as it arises."

—MARK J. HARRIGAN, *VP, Suffolk County National Bank*

"Get the F. out of my office. Your whining is really starting to piss me off."

—ANONYMOUS *(former) National Retail Chain Executive*

STICKY NEWS
EXTRA, EXTRA, READ ALL ABOUT IT!

Everyone's Scared of Employee Who Stares!

A faithful male employee complains to you (female PHP Manager), that his newer, fellow employee: stares and glares at him for long periods. And it really frightens him. You should …

A. Tell him to do it right back to him—stare him down!

B. Do nothing? There's no problem here. The complaining employee should ignore it.

C. Just keep an eye (no pun intended) on the situation?

D. Put up a "no staring" sign?

E. Have a private meeting with the other employees to get their take on it?

F. Punt?!

G. Have you noticed the choices expanding as the chapters progress? Is it beginning to kick in that there is really no correct answer—until you apply **PHP**?

You always knew there was something a bit strange about that employee, even during the interview. Nothing like super weird or anything, just well…different. Yet, he's been working out well for a while now; in fact, he just had his six-month review. All was well. You've heard the expression, "All good things must come to an end?" One of your best veteran employees comes to you, and tells you that the new person… stares. That's right, stares! He connects eyes and doesn't let go.

Remember the **THIMK** from Chapter Four: "Is it really a problem?" Why, you never heard of such a thing! You're tempted to tell your complaining employee (albeit one of your best) to go back to work and stop looking for such little problems! Most managers would say this is *not* a situation to address. Looking's for free, right?! But you, my dear manager, learned that in the harassment video (they showed you at work), that if something or someone at work bothers an employee, it IS your issue. Besides, if your good people are distracted, productivity could suffer.

Here's a strategic tidbit first (most managers do not use this, for they think it's not doing their jobs completely). Yet often, it's a better way of handling tricky issues. You may ask your employee if he would like to address the situation with the offender. He'll initially look at you funny, but after you explain to him that if/when you, the manager, talk to the offending employee, that person will know where (and from whom) it came from in the first place. You see, the manager will be tempted to share the origin; it could slip out. It often does. In some cases, there'll be an obligation to do so.

Most employees will decline the offer at this point. Some will even tell you to just forget the whole thing—subtly questioning your competence in handling the situation. Just assure your employee now, that you will indeed handle the dilemma. Because you will.

Let's prepare, shall we? You are a woman, and the complaining employee is a man, and so is the employee he is finding fault with. Should this matter? Maybe. But a **PHP** Manager always does the right thing, and does not allow him/herself to get bogged down with countless "what-if-ing." So remain objective, and carry on.

Just one or two other points to consider. Keep your eye on the goal. That is, you want everyone to work together smoothly. And remember, just as in any sticky predicament, address the **behavior** of the person, not the person. Are you ready? Are you scared? Of course you are. Uh oh, that four letter F-word is starting to creep in. FEAR! What if he's keeper of voodoo dolls? They always scared you as a kid! What if he's a powder keg, ready to blow? You know, you never really know what people are thinking! What if he knows where you live?!

Okay, relax. 'Time to **PHP** your way through this one. First: *PURITY.* This, you'll recall is being honest and APPRECIATIVE. You'll catch a tidbit of *HUMILITY* in there as well. Try it on for size.

> MANAGER: "Thanks for meeting with me, Stanley, I won't keep you long. There's something I need to bring to you attention. I feel a little awkward even bringing it up, but here goes. The first thing I want to let you know is that 'everyone' is not talking about it or anything like that. And please don't ask me where it came from, because I won't tell you, because it simply doesn't matter. If it were me, I would want someone to bring this to my attention. Stanley, you have a habit of staring at people. And it seems to spook them. This has almost nothing to do with your working, but more with the whole working environment for everyone involved."

One of the toughest things to do right now is to pause, but it's time. Enter: *PATIENCE.* Let the dust settle. See what he says. Okay, let's assume that rain buckets of silence enter the room. You feel your own pulse in various parts of your body. Stanley is now staring at you, arms folded—the glare in his eyes so powerfully blinding, you cannot even imagine a soul in there. It's question time, which hopefully will solicit answers. Or as we **PHP** Managers say, 'time to toss 'em the football...'

ACTION BRIEF! The person _asking questions_ is in control of the situation. Think twice about this one. It's a valuable tidbit.

MANAGER: "Like right now, Stanley, I'm afraid of what you're thinking about me—and what I said to you. What *are* you thinking?"

Now, sit back, maintain eye contact—and pause for the/an answer.

*THIMK! Let 'em see you sweat! Contrary to the old adage, the **HUMILITY** of letting someone "in," somehow encourages them to let down their guard. Maybe, just maybe, a more honest exchange of communication can now occur.*

Chances are that Stanley will say something now. What if he doesn't? Let **PHP** kick in. Chances are that your inner sense might direct you to try just one more time to toss him the football.

MANAGER: "Do you want to tell me what you're thinking, Stan? Did I offend you? That certainly was never my intention. (Pause; no response from Stanley).

IS this a surprise to you, Stan…or do you kind of know what I'm talking about? Are you thinking we can fix this problem from here? (Pause; still no response from Stanley). Stan, do you have anything else you'd like to say, at all? (Stan, with arms folded, now looking down, just shrugs a 'no'). I guess that's it then, Stan. I'll make some notes that we had this discussion, you can sign it to acknowledge that, or not. And I'll give you a copy if you want. ('Still nothing from Stanley). Okay, well thanks for your time, Stan."

Okay…confident manager—what's that you say? You're *not* confident it went smoothly? You blew it? You choked? Will he go and get a gun out of his trunk and…WOH! Stop!

First of all, this is your job. Managers are paid for the quality of their decisions. Were you honest with your employee? Sure you were (**PURITY**). You didn't dance around the topic, and as gingerly as you could: you jumped right into the sticky situation. This, my dear **PHP** Manager, is also demonstrating APPRECIATION. This is, as you recall, a key player in the *PURITY* cycle.

Your **HUMILITY** kept your ego at bay, when you ACCEPTED the fact that you felt awkward, and even letting Stan know you were a bit scared in discussing it. Why was Stanley staring? His mind is likely bogged down with some heavy thoughts. 'Money problems? 'Second job to fix those money problems—wearing on his home life? 'Wear and tear on his home life causing him to eat like crap, and not exercise any more? 'Concerned about his mother whose Alzheimer's is getting worse by the week? You can't fix these. **PHP** gives you super-powers, yes; but only Stanley's personal use of **PHP** can address those problems. You (**PHP** Manager) can help by creating and fostering a work environment that's emotionally safe and comfortable.

Consider these statistics from the May 2, 2007 issue of HR Executive (page 58; provided by LifeCare.com, Westport, Conn.), on the topic of "Work/Life Challenges." More than 1,500 U. S. Workers were asked to identify their greatest work/life challenge for the year. They responded:

31% Financial Issues

24% Work/Life Balance

12% Health and Wellness Matters

12% Other

10% Child Care Issues

8% Adult Care Issues

3% Legal Care Issues

So why was Stanley staring? What was going through his mind? What's he thinking right now? It almost doesn't matter to you. (Now that doesn't sound very nice, does it?!) Rephrased: it shouldn't matter too much to you. Why? Because it's out of your controllability.

The **PHP** Manager's task is to keep one and a half eyes on the ultimate goal: the problem itself; which in this case, is that Stan stares—and it scares other employees. Your goal is to cause this activity to cease. When it does, all parties involved will presumably have won. With this goal clearly before you, and then using ***PURITY, HUMILITY*** and ***PATIENCE***, the sticky situation will melt away. Guaranteed.

And all those questions boggling you before? When you use **PHP**, they will not even enter into your thoughts. You'll have no time any longer for "mind mischief." For **PHP** will begin to consume your energy. It's a beautiful thing.

HONING YOUR PHP INTUITION

PURITY, HUMILITY and ***PATIENCE*** are the keys for becoming proficient at using your inner sense. An old, anonymous adage says, "The beginning of wisdom is silence...the second stage is listening." In other words, shut up! Sit back. Chill. Newly-minted, green managers are anxious to talk, to get to that solution immediately.

But Kenny Rogers reminds us, "You got to know when to hold...know when to fold up." He was referring to gambling, but is life not unlike one, big poker game? Another colloquial expression is ***timing is everything***. Sometimes new managers can go to the other extreme with scary, **sticky** conflicts; procrastinating...putting off dealing with them as long as possible. Then again, a problem is simply a golden, unresolved opportunity.

Confused by the last couple paragraphs? Let's begin with a mantra, then work it from there. The apex of **Solving** Sticky *People Problems* is to "jump right into" a troubled situation. But the depth we dive, and the technique we use, will depend on our ***intuition.*** Jumping in means to immediately begin the thinking process. Some managers tune out the noise of problems. **PHP** Managers tune-in! Listen. Closely. Watch. Closely. You're not yet ready to consider ***how*** to address the situation. So much of the ideal **PHP** Management strategy is to simply wait...and watch—preserving a healthy distance. Separate enough to remain objective.

For instance, one of your favorite employees (okay, we shouldn't have faves—but we're human after all; some are just more likable than others!) comes to you complaining that another employee has been bullying her. Nothing major, just smart-alecy-type behavior. The quick tendency is to get our gander up, march right over to that bully...and give 'em an earful.

After all, you're the boss—nobody screws with you! You're operating from your ego.

The **PHP** reaction to this would be, "Man, I'm POed at this bully for being so mean to my fave employee. But I know that most of what I'd say right now would be emotional—***and*** would make it even more difficult for my fave employee; for it would create an underlying, angry atmosphere. A **PHP** Manager knows that bullies want to get a rise out of the people they're bullying—and their managers as well.

You may eventually have to talk to the bully about this behavior, but not when you're hot. ***PURE*** is not angry, or "I'll show him who's boss!" ***HUMBLE*** is not letting an inflated ego do your disciplining for you. And ***PATIENCE*** is WFFI, "Waiting for further instructions." This is the intuitive process. Yes, **PHP** Manager, your involvement might be needed, but not yet…maybe not ever.

Much evidence has been shown, that managers get waaaay too involved, waaay too quickly, in these matters. If we let things settle—under our watchful **PHP** eyes and ears, we will find that things have a way of working themselves out. Employees really can handle so many of their own battles (for lack of a better word): ***better*** without management intrusion. This is actually one of the tenets of effective delegation as well (Chapter Six). The joint (your company) should run even ***better*** when the **PHP** Manager is ***not*** there. 'Easier said than done getting to that point—but it's a worthy delegation goal. (**PHP** Note: Managing people is a lot like teaching students is a lot like raising children; it's about respect, it's about expectations. 'Repeating the previous point: ***easier said than done***, but a worthwhile aspiration just the same).

You read in previous paragraphs to "jump in!" yet sit back at the same time. Again, to clarify (because it is so vital)…**PHP** intuition is jumping in with a concerned, watchful observation. The sitting back part is allowing ***PURE, HUMBLE,*** and ***PATIENT*** thinking to kick in. When you do this, it'll feel like you're working less, but your level of effectiveness will sky rocket. Many managers these days believe that God (whatever you conceive Him to be) *is* **PHP** intuition. Gentleman Farmer

John M. Leuthardt says, "The business relationship will be better served if both parties live up to the person Christ wants them to be."

A **PHP** Manager ***gets ready***. Just as Derek Jeter gets set and planted at Shortstop, ready to lunge in all directions, so does a **PHP** Manager. Just as John Edwards gets set and prepared before a psychic reading (to protect himself from negatively draining the energy right out of him), so does a **PHP** Manager.

Think. Be conscious of using these powerful tools. Make a concerted effort to be ***PURE*** in mind and soul. Keep your !@#$%*& ego far away—realizing your ***HUMILITY.*** And be okay about ***PATIENTLY*** not knowing exactly what's going to happen next; even get excited in that suspense. Properly using **PHP** will nurture intuition. And your inner sense will always show you the correct strategies. It'll almost feel like you're cheating, but without the guilt.

Chapter 10

Disciplining and Firing—almost always *Sticky*

How to do it (when you have to): <u>safely</u> and <u>calmly</u> while staying out of court!

NOTES FROM THE PHP MANAGER'S JOURNAL...

"It is almost better to *break the law* but enforce your questionable employee policy across the board...than to keep to every letter of the law, and apply your policy inconsistently among your employees."

—NEW YORK STATE JUDGE, *Unemployment Law Division*

STICKY NEWS

EXTRA, EXTRA, READ ALL ABOUT IT!

"Hero Manager Fires Twelve Year Employee!"

Edward O' Sullivan is popular. When Eddie comes into work, chants ring out…"What's up Sully…?" "Suuuulllyyy…" (This last one complete with pointer/pinky/thumb rock-on symbol). Though you've been his manager for almost a year now, it still feels new. And you'll never be part of the ole' boy's club. That's just the way it is in this profitable, 60-employee medical billing company.

Eddie has stretched the bungee for appropriate behavior in the past nearly dozen years at MEDbill. When he dressed like a hooker for the Halloween bash, he stole the show. But the grapevine was buzzing with things like, "It was actually a little embarrassing looking at those fake breasts," which looked quite real and tawdry. But most chuckled and time passed. Then there was the time he hung Chippendale calendars in the women's lounge after hours. They eventually just came down. Many smiled and *apparently* wrote it off as, "Oh that Sully!"

(PHP Manager's Note: Notice the word *apparently* above. It'll be key in future discussions in this chapter).

But this time, this incident seems different—almost a little creepy. Okay, hang on there a minute, Skippy, we already know how the story ends—somebody gets canned, you know—layed off, excessed, terminated, let-go. Does Sully get fired in this story? And why did the headline say the manager was a hero who did the dirty deed? Read on. First, a bit of company background. We read it's a small to medium-sized officey/probably cubey-type environment. Get the visual in your minds—large number of women (your hint was that there's a lounge for them). Some probably dress more "appropriately" than others. Here is a page from the employee handbook.

(Extra bonus hint to follow this lengthening story: We now also know we'll be re-visiting two words: *apparently* and *appropriately*).

Dress Code Policy

We pride ourselves at MEDbill to always be appropriately attired for our clients, and as an example to each other. Business casual is the norm. Ties and sport coats are encouraged but not required. The business look for women encourages skirts with hosiery, but is not required. Not conforming to the standards will not be dismissal grounds necessarily, but could affect wage increases and promotions.

Page 17

Clear? Sure, as mud (or pea soup if you're hungry, or peanut butter if you enjoy watching the cartoon <u>Rudolph the Red Nosed Reindeer</u>). Oh it sounds fine—almost professional…hanging on words like pride, attired, conforming, and standards. Still with the story? And what the dickens does this have to do with Eddie O'Sullivan?

Sully (only God knows why) took it upon himself to count the number of female employees who wore "hose" during the month of July. Out of 43, 32 consistently wore dresses or skirts (number includes executives—Sully's bosses!). Out of those 32, 15 wore hosiery. Stay with me as the numbers are confusing. Simple math tells us that 17 female employees *did not* during the month of July, 2010 wear anything on their legs.

"So what?" you're thinking. "Who cares?" Well, Sully took an interest in a slightly overweight, 28 year-old, clerical assistant named Regina. She was one of the 17 "naked-leggers" as Sully referred to his survey sample. Everyone at MEDbill gets reviewed in July. Regina (fake name, BTW) was the only one who was asked to start wearing hosiery. How did Sully know all this? He asked…*everyone.*

Sully drafted a note to the principals of the company. It asked a question to the effect: that concerning a "dress code breach," how can most ladies be okay, but one is not? In other words, why was Regina being singled out? Sully's memo essentially suggested that MEDbill keep to the policy and enforce it across the board; or examine the no-bare policy and perhaps change it. Management's knee-jerk reaction to the memo? Sully should MYOB (mind *his* own business, that is). But **PHP** Managers are not knee-jerks. So thinking with *PURITY*, is there anything *true* in the memo? Is there *integrity* and *validity in what he's enthusiastically* posing? Egotistical executives would fire him immediately, dismissing any and all of his ideas. *HUMBLE* execs stop and think. *PATIENT* Managers step back to consider all options—the whole picture. They *wait for further instructions.*

There's a barrel full of stuff going on here. The **PHP** process is almost never fast, but step-by-step. The sequence in which we proceed is key to successful handling of an issue.

THIMK! There are no real <u>problems</u> in managing people…only golden, unresolved, pending <u>opportunities</u>—to make work life better!

Step One. Decide if there is a true problem here. One **PHP** Manager uses this litmus test: "If it just affects me, bothers me personally, it still may *not* be a problem with which I need to deal. If the problem whatever it may be affects even one other employee, I need to deal with it in some way, albeit small."

Step Two. What is the outcome we desire at the end of the day, so to speak? Answer, not necessarily in this order…for Regina to wear hosiery; for Sully to stop surveying employees on personal matters; to have clarity in policy interpretation (in this case, dress code).

Scene Two—results so far…after Regina's review, she began wearing hosiery. She looked ten times better and apparently just wanted to be a cooperative, company person; and probably desired to look as good as possible as well. Problem solved? So it would seem so far.

Scene Three—Eddie Sully…following is a close excerpt of the way a disciplinary action started.

*ACTION BRIEF! Whenever possible, stay away from using the word "discipline" when conversing with employees. It has nothing but negative connotations in life. How to avoid it? Just DON'T USE IT. Your **PHP** intuition will automatically slot in substitute wording.*

MANAGER: "Good morning, Eddie. Thanks for stopping in. I wanted to talk to you about the whole survey thing…dress code situation, talking to the girls, blah-blah-blah."

EDDIE: "Blah-blah-blah? Sounds like you're thinking it's no big deal!"

MANAGER: "Weeeelllll, I hope we can make it *not* a big deal…"

EDDIE: "Huh?"

MANAGER: "Ed, you know (progressively louder voice) you should have kept your nose out of the girls' business, both Regina and everyone else you involved in this ridiculous…this wild…survey thing about something so persona…"

EDDIE: (Interrupting and mirroring the increased volume of his manager) "Do you even understand the issue here? You guys are picking on a poor, defenseless fat girl, who has white piano calves—telling her to cover them up, while (unintentional pause as Eddie begins to lose his breath a little as his mouth dries and anger builds) the rest of the hot, little chicks go around here bare-legged, yet nobody gives a #$%^ because they're…you… are turned on checkin' 'em out. Fix the ^&*% problem or you're gonna' get it fixed for you in Human Rights Court!" (Eddie leaves abruptly).

*THIMK! What is the four-letter, "F" word in every **PHP** Manager's tool box? F ___ ___ ___.*

Eddie, like most employees (especially if they're also human) wants only one thing: fairness and consistency. **PHP** Managers set the pace and tone of their workplace culture. Treat employees equally, administer instructions fairly; your employees will treat each other accordingly. You could be the most neurotic individual in the world, but your people don't see you that way. Your employees are somewhat blinded by the fact that they view you as the *stable* one—the balancer in their lives. You don't even think you deserve it. But as Mary Kay Ash said, "Fake it until you make it." She was not suggesting being insincere—but psyching one's self up; playing the part!

Remember your hero of yesteryear? Superman, Batgirl, your older sister or brother? Heroes are always *on*, never sporadic in their behavior (at least to those who admire them). You can be a minor hero to your employees simply by operating calmly and consistently. Flare-ups *do not* have to occur "every so often." Having a temper tantrum is just a bad habit. Replace it with a hero habit.

(**PHP** Bonus Visual: close your eyes and envision a work environment always calm and perpetually peaceful. Courts and lawsuits are ancient terms. It's always sunny and everyone is smili…OKAY ENOUGH OF THIS, BACK TO WORK).

ACTION BRIEF! Be consistent. Heroes are.

So back to the meeting (a couple paragraphs ago) with Eddie. Went well, huh? Not. (Here's how it *should have played* out). Take two:

> **MANAGER:** "Good morning, Eddie. Thanks for stopping in. I wanted to talk to you about the dress code situation, Regina, future policy implementation, and so on. If you don't mind, let me share my thoughts first just for a few minutes, and then we can have an open conversation. Sound okay?"

(**PHP** Manager's Quickie Strategic Analysis: If Eddie chooses to jump in here and begin talking even though asked to wait, exercise *PATIENCE*. Let him talk. It'll be worse if he keeps it bottled up inside. And notice another piece of sage advice: never demand of someone…what you can ask of them as a favor).

> (**EDDIE** nods his head to signify "Okay.")

> **MANAGER:** "First, we applaud your interest in trying to help. That may sound strange coming from me, but what I mean is,

you're attempting to make a situation better—and maybe more people should at least bear that outlook on life here at MEDbill. I guess, and I say I guess cause I'm really not sure if there's a better way or not (*HUMILITY*), another approach…possibly a preferred approach would have been to come to me first with how you felt about things, what you saw, etc. (Manager moving slowly, not ahhing or uhming, but letting **PHP** guide the words) Not really sure how I would have proceeded (*PURITY, HUMILITY*), but the whole discussion likely would not be as big as it became."

(EDDIE crosses his arms…maybe readying himself to jump in defensively?).

This is a crucial **PHP** moment. You don't know which direction this conversation may or will take. Don't rush. If Sully engages in the discussion now, you'll hear him and reply in full **PHP** color. If not, the *right* words will continue to come from you. (Reminder of the process: *when* you're being truly *PURE* and truly *HUMBLE* and truly *PATIENT*, it's impossible to say or do the wrong thing. Stay **PHP**, and the inner sense will keep working. It's guaranteed. Believers: keep on keeping on. Skeptics: just *trust* as you're *trying* to get it. You will.

Assuming you still have the floor though, you may continue with…

MANAGER: "As far as Regina goes, and the way we address the dress code from here on, I promise you—we will focus on being more sensitive and fair and consistent. Also, we do plan to clarify the policy. The intention is actually to just help all of us look as good as we can, because our clients (and higher-ups, and everyone frankly) judge books by their covers. Doesn't seem fair but it's real. We like Regina very much and value her as a fine employee, but it's probably better I say as little as possible about her at this point…as all employees should have a modicum of privacy and confidentiality. I'm not saying to mine/mind your own beeswax, Eddie, because I know you're just trying to help.

Just that I am sensitive to the situation, glad it came to our attention, and promise to address it from here."

(**DISNEY** Dream World Response) Eddie: "Well, thanks. Let me know what else I can do to help."

Happy ending? Maybe. Maybe not. As Harry Chapin used to say, "You musicians in the audience will notice we have gone to a minor key...the plot is thickening!" Okay, Regina's situation is hunky-dory—in good shape. But in relooking at the dress code policy, do you want to say, "Hefty chicks who do not have tan legs should cover them up" (?!) Of course not, but that's the desired outcome.

(**PHP** Brainstorm Idea: Put together a focus group of a mix of employees, share with them the *desired outcome* (obviously not as graphically as the previous paragraph), and get their feedback on rewriting the policy. This is MBO in action (remember seeing this in a few other chapters?). Is this idea **PURE** and **HUMBLE? PATIENCE** may very well be needed when you see what the task force comes up with, but you're ready).

Screwball: In the process of implementing the above idea, it came to your attention that a number of people were skeeved (actual word used twice) by Sully asking them if their reviews stated anything about their bare legs. The result: Nine women employees, two men who even contributed their two cents, *and* a concerned e-mail from a husband of another female employee. The common word used here was "uncomfortable." One woman said, "I avoid all contact with Sully—now more than ever." Another shared, "If Eddie's in the lounge at lunch, we just go back to our desks." And yet another shared (confidentially, of course), "He turns my stomach; I can't even look at him. I get a sick feeling coming to work now."

Holy cow! Nothing should shock you, but man-oh-Manaschevitz, you are! Sexual harassment polices are generally based on legal phrasing which says to the effect, that in cases of harassment, the manager/company is at fault if they knew about it; or (and this is a big "or") *should have known.* That translates to: We managers have to stay on top of all the communication going on in our plants, stock rooms, warehouses, retail floors, showrooms, farm fields…you get the picture.

SEXUAL HARASSMENT COMES IN TWO FLAVORS

"Quid pro quo" is one type. It means "this for that" which often consists of requested *favors* by higher-up managers. The other general category is known as "Hostile work environment." Basically, it's when people feel uncomfortable. MEDbill is presently living in a hostile work environment.

Thinking back, could Sully's Halloween costume have helped to promote this…*environment?* Yes, it's possible. Possible that it made others feel *uncomfortable*. What about when he hung the hunky calendars… hostile work environment? Yes, it's probable. Just because there were no complaints does not take us out of the woods. Remember the wording— we *should have known*.

So now what? Should you connect with your higher-ups and maybe just terminate Sully? Is it that serious? He'd be surprised! And generally speaking, in employee relations, there should be no surprises. Does his twelve-year tenure deserve a conversation? You decide to talk with him, just to share what you're thinking and prevent/alleviate as much "uncomfort" as possible in the company.

> **MANAGER:** "Good morning, Eddie. I want to just bring something to your attention which I believe is problematic— maybe even more so than either of us is aware. I'm going to get right to it (**PURITY**). A number of employees here feel and are uncomfortable around you. Please don't ask me names, because it's not wise to share the information at this point. And I also request that you not even discuss this meeting with any other employees. I'm telling you this because I would want to know it if it were me—so I could try to stop the bad feelings some people are having. It seems like everything from the risque' Halloween costume a few years ago; to hanging up the Chippendale pictures;

and most recently, polling the employees on what they wear. I do want you to know that *everyone is not talking behind your back* or anything like that—probably because most people like you. But the things you've done make some feel uncomfortable. I wasn't sure if I should even have this conversation with you (**HUMILITY**), or what if any next steps should be taken (?) (Manager surprised at the lack of any response from Sully). Just wanted to make you aware. (Pause). 'Any thoughts? Comments? Suggestions? (Another pause).

EDDIE: "Nope, that it?"

MANAGER: "Yeah…I…guess so. Thanks for your ti—" (Eddie out of his chair even before manager finished the sentence).

Nothing like second guessing, huh? But when you know in your heart that you've done the *right thing*, every response is fine. It's almost as if the situation must take on a life of its own; evolve. We are *not* in full control of every situation (**HUMILITY**). You've done what you believe and feel is good, true, and beautiful. Now chill a bit. (**PATIENCE**).

Four days pass and it all begins to feel like business as usual. You're still torn between soliciting information from employees, like "How's it going around Sully, lately?" or just letting it die. Fortunately or not, sometimes we receive life prompts to help us decide—like a supervisory MapQuest. There it is…marked "Confidential" and addressed to you! The contents included a page from the manual, and another representing a petition of sorts.

Sexual Harassment Policy

Employees at MEDbill will treat everyone with the utmost courtesy and respect.

We pride ourselves in maintaining an environment free of harassment of any kind, where all employees can work comfortably together.

Page 26

MEMO TO: (your name)

FROM: "Concerned Employees" (our signatures are below)

DATE: (today)

TOPIC: Edward O' Sullivan

We, the undersigned do not feel comfortable working around the above-mentioned person. Though he's likeable, he pries into the personal business of others, and we don't really trust him.

His presence working here makes it very hard for us to do our jobs properly. Please keep this confidential.

Thank you.

Wow. Seems like there's no choice, but to can the guy. There's always a choice though, and always options.

THIMK! *Fence-sitting and other wishy-washy behaviors will drain your energy quicker than many other things. But* <u>*when*</u> *you decide, your new commitment escalates—dramatically!*

ACTION BRIEF! *Think. Think hard. Think again. Go back and forth. Should I, shouldn't I? What's the worst possible case either way? Write down pros and cons for each. Be flexible in your analysis. Then decide with no turning back. Then work like heck to insure that you succeed in that direction you chose.*

Decision-making involves everything a manager does in his or her daily life. Whether the problem is minute or monumental, managers are paid for the *quality of their decisions.* Why? Because decisions involve risk, especially when possible outcomes are uncertain. When a **PHP** Manager decides something, especially if it is controversial, it's important to stick with it. That's why the risk factors are weighed in early on. Kenny Rogers told us that real gamblers, "Know when to hold, know when to fold up, know when to walk away, know when to run." The band, The Clash simplified it even further asking, "Should I Stay or Should I Go?"

In another instance, just because the employee *shows up* (even late)—in an environment of not being able to hire good help…is *not* a reason *not* to fire someone. Even in the case of a child care center, which is required by law to maintain a certain ratio of employees to children: the children's welfare is too important to keep around a problem employee. You may even temporarily lose a client(s) because of not keeping to the mandated ratios. But it's the right thing to do. Let 'em go.

So the thinking process begins. Sit quietly somewhere, free of distractions. Around water for about twenty minutes, if possible, will be a great investment in time. Twelve years is a long time these days for an employee to keep a job. What will Sully do? He still probably has at least 20 years left to work before retirement (somewhere). Has a family. Yup, would really stink for him. But you know it'll be better for many at the company—they already told you that in the confidential note. Sure, it's an *opportunity* to potentially change things for the better at MEDbill; but again, what about Sully?

Now try this. Become quiet—no more questions. Let your powerful mind think only *PURE* thoughts—APPRECIATING everything about the company, the employees (including Sully), and your own job. Allow your *HUMILITY* to drive out any egotistical mind games—for this could mean doing things for the wrong reasons. This could include looking whimpy in front of your co-workers on tough decisions. The "right thing" is often hidden. Be *PATIENT* with that fact, as things may not appear pleasant immediately. And furthermore, *PATIENCE* is virtuous throughout this entire process…dealings with Eddie, your higher-ups, other employees. And perhaps especially, with yourself. Good and helpful supervisors like ourselves frequently neglect "us." Being *PATIENT* and kind to self, gives continual strength for the **PHP** journey.

And so you sit on the proverbial fence of what to do with this employee. You think. You use **PHP**. Your normal, everyday, plain vanilla human emotions cloud the issue. You use **PHP** again. And finally, it's clear—you know what to do.

(**PHP** Manager's Note: The outcome is unknown until the above process occurs. It cannot be short-circuited. Many try. Please don't.).

Back to our regularly-scheduled-program. In the case solely on which this chapter is based, the decision was made to terminate Eddie's employment with MEDbill. As has been stated numerous times in this book, there should be no *surprises* in communicating with employees. Warnings given within the progressive discipline policy should be administered consistently at the company. This is so employees can *change their behaviors to improve their performance*, according to company guidelines, policies, and procedures. (The previous wording is effective; feel free to understand it clearly first, and then use it). In this case however, there is substantial reason and evidence that harassment (specifically a hostile work environment) has occurred. Part of the due diligence is <u>verifying with each individual employee who signed the memo—privately.</u> If there appears to be peer pressure of any substance, more **PATIENCE** and more diligence is in order. In the actual case on which this is based, each individual employee offered similar accounts. "We didn't want to have to do it" was a common thread. "We don't dislike Eddie—even feel badly for him" was another. "But he just makes us *uncomfortable*. We are afraid of what he'll say or do next." Research-gathering meetings also surfaced that similar behaviors, albeit more subtle, have been going on for years.

Employees being uncomfortable — alone is good reason to fire him. But that same uncomfort is likely affecting productivity in ways you'll never be able to measure. Harassment is in the eye of the beholder. A key point here is that even if you take this situation through the progressive discipline procedures...and even *if* Eddie flies right, damage is done. And may continue to be done as long as he's there. If they (employees) think/ feel they're being harassed, they probably are. It is clear he has to go.

MANAGER: "Eddie, I have bad news. It will even shock you. But I'm going to get right to it. Then we can discuss all the whys."

EDDIE: (With eyebrows crunching, almost bracing) "G'head."

MANAGER: "We are terminating your employment as of now. The reason is because you have created a hostile work environment. It's a type of sexual harassment. Specifically, your action over the past few years—especially the past few months have made employees feel uncomfortable. Please don't ask me who they are, because I won't specifically name them. But I will add that there's not one person who *does not* like you; and they will, as I do, feel very badly about this outcome. The work environment simply cannot remain in a state of uncomfortable employees. It's most counter productive. (Eddie just looking at manager, not glaring but almost a blank stare; manager pauses for any comments). Shall I continue? Do you want to say anything? (No reaction from Eddie). I don't know what you're thinking or feeling, Eddie. I wish there was another way to handle this situation. Still not sure this is the best way, but I'm trying. I thought about it long and hard, to make it as less shocking and terrible for you as possible."

(Observation Note: All the thought the **PHP** Manager has invested is being fully realized in this "monologue." The **PURITY** is flowing, **HUMILITY** is abundant. And **PATIENCE** will continue to be needed as it goes into the next phase of conversation).

MANAGER: "We're paying you until the end of the cycle, Eddie—that's 'til a week from this Friday. Here's the check. HR will be following up with you on the COBRA paperwork and a couple other exit documents. I wrote it all up, Eddie. (Manager gently slides a copy of the termination document across the desk). You can initial it if you don't mind, just to acknowledge that we had the conversation. You can write something on it. And you can have a copy as well. (Eddie glancing at document). Any questions, thoughts?"

EDDIE: "That it?"

MANAGER: "Yes. You can leave now. I had your personal items packed up from your desk. They're by the Security Exit. Also, I want you to know that in about an hour, I'll be putting out an e-mail blip simply stating that Eddie O' Sullivan is no longer with MEDbill, and which people will be doing the work until we replace you…which will not be easy at all."

(**EDDIE** goes into one of his famous Sully smiles…he calls it a banana grin, and says) "You're right, boss, I screwed up. And it's absolutely the right thing to do in canning me. I would too. And the two weeks pay? I don't even deserve it. You've been the greatest boss I've ever ha…" (Woh, bucko! What are you smokin', man? It ain't gonna' happen! Maybe eventually everyone will live happily ever after, but not yet; not today).

(Alternate Ending Number Two: "The Real Deal"…Eddie begins folding the paper even as he's still sliding it across the desk, completing the process right into his breast pocket. He walks out the door without a word).

No second guessing! You did the right, real thing. He fired himself. He'll be replaced. But you almost wish he'd expressed some kind of emotion—silence was so out of his character. What's he thinking? Does he have a machine gun in the trunk of his car?! OMG!

Were you fair? Consistent? *PURE, HUMBLE* and *PATIENT*? Did you APPRECIATE everything about Eddie and the meeting going as smoothly as it did? Did you/do you ACCEPT the fact that whatever happens from here—you did the right thing? Your *inner sense* has guided you throughout the process. It has worked, all of it. The correct outcome is inevitable. You feel it…still temporarily somewhat sad for Eddie, but okay because you know it's all under control.

(**PHP** Manager Age/Gender Considerations: There should be *none*. Courtrooms and political speeches are filled with set-ups and contrived outfits, expressions, who looks more believable, and so on; like "If we have a young, female prosecutor…" "If we have an older white-haired candidate…" This all works from a marketing standpoint, and **PHP** Managers should be aware of glaring problems of inappropriate situations. But all that being said, if you are **PHP** Managing, it doesn't matter who's old, who's which gender, blah, blah, blah. Effective messages will always be communicated when **PURITY, HUMILITY** and **PATIENCE** are active.

WHAT IS THE BEST DAY OF THE WEEK TO FIRE AN EMPLOYEE?

There's much disagreement on the answer to this question. "No day" is the best one. Yet when the dirty deed has to be done, it ain't Friday—that's for certain. This is emphasized because many people think it is. Try this on for size if you gotta' do it. If you let them go on a Tuesday morning around 10:30ish, they're shocked, POed, and they'll have a rotten afternoon. That's pretty much guaranteed. Tuesday evening won't be much better as they'll have a rough time on the home front as well. Wednesday morning, they'll still be very upset—maybe not having slept at all either. By that next afternoon, they'll almost start to consider options, "What will I do now?" By family dinner time on Wednesday evening, the shock value has stabilized. They're not happy obviously, but the big clouds are beginning to give way to some clearing. By Thursday morning (and this is assuming you've done the firing fairly, consistently, and legally—meaning you've followed all your company's policies), they'll even be thinking about their next move for another job. By Friday, they may even be beginning the process; the weekend's not that sucky after all. But you know what…it would be if they had gotten their rear-end canned on Friday afternoon! This advice will keep you out of court more often as well. Even if you win in court, you've already lost. You don't even want to be there.

PROPERLY <u>DISCIPLINING</u> AND <u>FIRING</u>
SHOULD FEEL LIKE...

A Hundred and One Things that Feel Good!

 # 37: *"It's been a great summer! Swimming everyday for hours means that all is well with the world when you're eight years old. But will that* *annoying ear clog ever clear? The left one did almost immediately. But it's been over a day on the right one. And then...when you least expect it! Oooooooohhhhh! Sooo quiet, sooo warm—to this day you still don't know what that fluid flowing down into the bottom of your ear was all about. Yet you'll never forget how clear and clearing it felt."*

SECTION C

The Sticky Challenge of **Balancing**
—Work, Home and Health—
...in a world of change

Chapter 11

Managing Energy, Time and *Sticky Stressors* (in that order) for TOTAL BALANCE! *YES*, it really IS possible

NOTES FROM THE PHP MANAGER'S JOURNAL...

"If I had to give one word, it would be COMPROMISE!!!! We are a service-based industry, so we need to be at work on time and in a fantastic frame of mind to provide our clients with the best experience.

99

In order to achieve this I have found that we need to be flexible but fair Re. time off, vacation, and the like...SO...we try to arrange... Everyone is happy, the (Client appointment) book is full and life is beautiful, as we know it at T. Carlton's!!!

LOL!!! Honestly, we do the same for many unexpected days off... kids, school trips, concerts, we don't get much notice of these kind of things, and as a parent, I understand the importance of being there as much as I can...as well as having to work...so I will always compromise when possible, it's what has always worked for us!!!"

—CHRISTINE CARLTON, *Owner, T. Carlton's Spalon, St. James, NY*

STICKY NEWS
EXTRA, EXTRA, READ ALL ABOUT IT!

Grumpy Manager Gets Home, Does Not Speak Through Dinner, Crashes on Sofa at 6:30!

You arrive home from your supervisory position at 5:45 PM. You mentally plan your evening: serve dinner, clean-up, kids homework, do bills, use the extra hour or so to touch up the trim in the bathroom (dinner party coming up this weekend).

You figure you'll have until about tenish to get all this in. But right after dinner, you feel WIPED! 'Drained! Now, you don't even feel like cleaning up. You should ...

A. Leave it for the morning—just get up earlier?

B. Make coffee, push-push-push yourself—you lazy clown, you!

C. Get mad at yourself for always letting yourself get to this feeling? It's the only way to change things.

D. Hit the tube and the sofa, man! You're spent! 'Can't fool your own body.

E. Read this chapter.

Well, that doesn't sound like a dreadful headline now, does it? Go to work, get home, chow down, chill, hit the hay, get up, go to work, get ho…well, okay…maybe it's not everyone's idea of excitement. But you know, work is work, that's why we call it work! Take another look at the headline. Let's take it, blow by blow. First, why is the manager coming home grumpy, then being quiet, then just "crashing?" To answer the question, let's rewind and play out the day, shall we?

Here's Tamara's planner for Tuesday. Tamara is a first-line supervisor at an electronics-manufacturing firm. She's part of one of the many support departments—invoices, communications, and general paperwork flow.

To Do List

Thursday, November 19th

6:00 AM — make sure Samantha's V-ball uni is clean!!

— call vet to see if Jasper- picked up today or tomorrow (post surgery)

7:00 AM — (cereal with wheat germ today, NO bagel!!!!)

8:00 AM

9:00 AM — call Josh's science teacher (why doing so poorly?!!)

10:00 AM — STAFF MEETING 'til 11:00

11:00 AM — meet with Jameson (he wants to go over new procedures) ("some changes" ???!!)

NOON — lunch with Asshole to work out kids' new schedule (who has what weekends/holidays)

1:00 PM — call Dr. Prellan (why these stomach pains??!!)

— e-mail Mom and Dad (re: kids don't want to stay there for Christmas ☺)

— e-mail Pastor Beirne (can't come to meeting, but what want me to do to help?)

2:00 PM — meet with Val (she "has some concerns" ?!)
3:00 PM — 3:15 Supervisor's Weekly Meeting
4:00 PM — Video Conf.: "Change in the Workplace"
5:00 PM — Catch end of Sammie's game!
6:00 PM — Mac/cheese/hot dogs
7:00 PM — Josh- Kung Fu lesson, 7:30

Yes, Tamara is busy. But so are you. She's smart, and a good planner, excellent organizer. And so are you. (I know that because you're reading this book!). You believe in helping yourself—in getting better. Let's objectively analyze Tamara's day. You undoubtedly see yourself somewhere in her shoes. Starting with Samantha's team uniform, Sammie is almost ten. So what exactly is the age when kids start assuming responsibility for such things? 'Fact is: most ten year olds don't, but what wears Tammie down is *thinking about it!* Tammie's mother says her grandchildren are spoiled. Then again, ten-year-old girls didn't even play competitive volleyball thirty years ago. Tammie's mother didn't quite understand, but that didn't alleviate Tammie's "single-mother guilt." Okay, we're showing energy drainage already, and it's not even eight AM!

Analysis Note: Washing clothes is easy, but the feeling of guilt in any form, is wearing. And Tammie's mom pours it on. But the only reason it's a problem is that Tammie thinks too much about it; this causes her to "hide" these tasks from her mother—creating a push-pull among pleasing her daughter, pleasing her mother, and pleasing herself. Marcia G. Rosen (M.Rosen Consulting, www.mrosenconsulting.com) shares "It's essential to know when you have to *unglue yourself* from sticky people! Your success and sanity may well depend upon it." 'Remember Ricky Nelson's song about the party at the Garden? He said it's not possible to please everyone. So you have to please yourself.

THIMK! *Guilt has no place in the* **PHP** *toolbox. We're <u>always</u> working for ourselves first and foremost.*

Whoa, cowboy, that doesn't sound very **PHP**ish—sounds a little selfish actually. Here's the rub. **PHP** Managers *always* do the right thing.

When you use **PHP**, you can't help but do the right thing. <u>When</u> this occurs, you become exempt from others' opinions. It's like when you fly, and the attendant instructs you to put on your own oxygen mask first, **then** attend to your small children. You must take care of #1 first.

ACTION BRIEF! Make YOU happy consistently.

So back to Tammie…when her mom questions her parenting, she'll smile and say, "Thanks, Mom!" Then, she keeps doing her own thing. By the way, an aside goal of **PHP** Managing is quietly and gently sharing the principles with others. There's truth to the adage that the best way to learn something is to teach it. So don't be surprised if your mom learns in the process. **PHP** Managers steadily indoctrinate "life lessons" on everyone they meet daily—delicately and non-judgmentally.

ACTION BRIEF! Immediately put EVERYTHING into perspective. How important is IT…in the general scheme of life?

THIMK! What is it: that's causing the hemorrhage of energy?

Let's go back to the "To Do List" page. 'Second item: checking on the dog. Can this be delegated? Could/should Tammie's ex-husband do this? After all, it IS the kids' pet. Oh sure, Josh feeds him; but half the time, Tammie has to remind him. Use **PHP**, and you will see that managing people and raising children are incredibly similar. Employees are simply grown-up (most of the time!) kids! Calling the veterinarian remains in Tammie's duties. She should ACCEPT it totally—and not become distracted that she **wishes** her ex would take more responsibilities with the kids. Giving it thought chips away at the "expense side" of her *energy* "income statement." It drains her. Further, she should APPRECIATE the fact that her twelve-year-old son—feeds Jasper half the time; and does well in most of his school-work (though Science seems to present a challenge). Whew! We're not even at work yet!

Tammie's note reminding herself to eat healthier? Many of you know that if you commit something to paper, somehow…sometimes, it tends to become realized. Just the task of writing it down, then glancing at it: helps you to achieve it. So if indeed, Tammie does eat Multi-Grain Cheerios (to help keep her cholesterol in check), she may feel better about *going into her next meal*. In other words, lunch might just be healthier, simply because some momentum has been built. It's just like the first day of any diet being tough, the second day is often harder. By the third, you're thinking, "This really might work." Nothing succeeds like success. (This same philosophy goes for healthier family dinners as well).

Ain't no way we could analyze Tamara's entire day by micromanaging her To Do List. Well, we could actually, but we won't. For **PHP** is as personal as a fingerprint. When you apply it and live it, the execution is as individual and unique—as it is powerful. So let's merely hit some general hot spots, shall we? (This chapter takes a turn at this point. Disclaimer: the next few pages will "send" the reader to several other chapters in the rest of the book. It's not meant to serve as a tease, but more a review of what we've discovered).

Staff meeting at 10:00 AM…see Chapter Eight. Maybe you won't even need this meeting?! Meet with new boss at 11:00…he's keeping Tammie in suspense with "some changes." She could partially control her anxiety by asking him some additional details, so as to more effectively prepare for the meeting. To *Manage Change* in a **Sticky** World, we must unearth how to embrace it, and see it as only golden, unresolved opportunities! You know that just changing for just change sake, is silly. And you know that Jameson (new boss) goes directly to your employees, bypassing you. This meeting he called, is Tammie's opportunity to address this (using **PHP** of course). Should *you* be responsible for teaching *your* boss to be a **PHP** Manager? No. But might it make your work environment more pleasant?

Ah, yes, the Noon lunch with the kids' dad…Tammie's "X." Who takes the kids, when? You may want to recheck Chapter Two…Planning *Smooth Schedules…* How to use this tool for minimum **stickiness** and maximum efficiency. And make all your employees happy too! In this case, change that to make all your ex-husbands happy too! PS. Calling them names helps nothing or no one. Who needs the extra negativity?!

Let's go back to 9:00 AM, as the task seemed to get away from Tammie: Calling her son's science teacher and sending two e-mails in the afternoon (these are items that can be done pretty much anytime). **PHP** suggests simply asking questions…"I'm a bit concerned about Josh's Science grades. What can I do at home to help him to try and get them up?" Then—STOP! Tammie has tossed the football to the other party, **with a question**…non-confrontational, not long-winded. Some type of answer, hopefully followed by a dialogue will occur; and with that (optimistically)—an initial solution.

Sending out **sticky** e-mails to the parentals and the pastor…Tammie is learning to take her time with bad news. We should all read them over again, not only for grammar, spelling and punctuation, but for effect. How will it be taken? Could it be perceived this way? That way? Write it and rewrite it if you have to. Engaging **PHP** will insure safe and productive communication. By the way, advising Pastor Beirne that she cannot attend the meeting, but offering other help, is a great way to say "No" to requests. It's so much more **PHP** than fabricating excuses…or even going and feeling rushed and guilty, and doing a half-hearted job.

Hey, hold on there all you **PHP**ers! Should managers be conducting personal business at work? Would you do it if your boss were right there over your shoulder?

Here's an interesting stat from Office Team of Menlo Park, CA, which appeared in Human Resource Executive® magazine, as compiled by Michael O'Brien. It's titled *That's Personal* and reads, "Women said they take an average of 29 minutes daily to attend to personal tasks during office hours, while men admitted to 44 minutes daily, according to a survey of 559 U. S. adult workers and 150 senior executives." Tammie uses **PHP** to answer that question for herself. 'As we should.

Wow, 2:30 already?! What the heck could Valerie want to meet about? All she said was she had some concerns. Here's some background for the reader. Val is a long-time employee. She's been passed over (what seems like many) times for promotion. Val represents the typical employee who everyone likes, but can just never see—in a supervisory role. In fact, Tammie was the one who "bumped" her most recently. JFK said that

"Jealousy has killed more people than cancer." If you've ever been jealous (or even human!), you know how uncontrollable a feeling it is. Both you and Tammie will discover help on this in Chapter Three…Keeping High Quality/High **Productivity**/ High Morale…Help your employees to **destickyize** their own work—high performance will result!

But what if Val *did not* call for a meeting to air out her problems and issues? Instead, her mood-swinging demeanor untwined about the whole office—creating chaos. You might begin with, "Val, I'm sensing you're not feeling quite right today; your work is fine, but you don't seem happy. 'Not that you have to be bubbling over with sacchariney-sweet enthusiasm, but your sighing and little bit of eye-rolling is wearing on the rest of the crew a bit. And frankly, it might be wearing on you too, Val."

Val could either say she has no idea what you're referring to (even though your words *did* sink in, but she's too embarrassed to agree with you about her behavior). She could also say nothing (here again, your brief statement probably did penetrate). Regardless of the reaction (or lack thereof), the **PHP** Manager can gently assure their employee that they're *concerned not only about the flow of work from all the employees, but from the energy that's flowing around the office—positive or negative* (**PURITY**).

"Well, I don't want to stay stuck on it, Val…but if there's anything I can do to help personally or professionally, please don't hesitate to let me know." Even if Val simply says *thanks* or even nothing (be **PATIENT** with her), you have still done your job. You've made impact, even if you don't realize it (be **PATIENT** with you). **PHP** Managers *always do the right thing* (even those above or below you do not). Don't count on anyone telling you, 'Ya dun good!' In most cases, it ain't gonna' happen. So don't look for it (**HUMILITY**). Amazingly, your *inner sense* will provide you with the stamp of approval.

PHP Manager PS: Even though it shouldn't have to be the supervisor's job to be concerned about moods, we certainly can help to speed the process of "getting over it." Our biggest concern, however (truly our only concern) is *productivity* in the workplace. Employees fall into funks for reasons mostly unrelated to work, but **PHP** Managers serve the whole person—simply by keeping a close eye on the productivity ball.

If Val never confesses she's pissed off because she was passed over for promotion, you *may* want to address the issue in another way. You can always re-open the conversation and explain to her about how the company continually looks to put round pegs in round holes, and how it's normally tough to choose. Often, the only criterion employees truly understand is seniority—"If I'm there longer, I should make more money and get promoted." Fortunately or not, this is less valid than ever before. PS: There's that case for productivity again—employees measuring and motivating themselves…knowing rewards come on the heels of performance, not longevity.

Some employees will need more coaching on this cultural change more than others (**PATIENCE**). And your diligence in this process will not only accommodate and support change, but will *encourage* it as well. Not change for its own sake; but to nurture a safe culture of change as excitement—always looking for better approaches, formulas, programs! Remember, embracing problems as golden, unresolved opportunities.

The 3:15 and 4:00 o'clock meetings do not require much activity from Tammie. This doesn't mean sticking **PHP** in the top drawer. While you're sitting in a meeting, and someone is presenting, and it bugs you, use discretion. An example of this is the time Tammie's new boss sat there and told everyone that he "And Tamara have been spending countless hours on the new appraisal plan." Tammie wanted to blurt out, "Was I there?!!" Instead, she was discrete. It was easy when she recalled from Chapter Seven:

ACTION BRIEF! *Always do the right thing, even when those above you and below you, may not.*

You, the **PHP** reader, may be wondering why we bypassed discussing Tammie's call to her physician. Much data is coming to the forefront on associating pains (stomach, head, neck…you name it!)—to thought. Tammie places some faith in this theory; for she has her pains: Monday through Friday. That's why she frequently writes a note to herself to call her doctor, but as yet—has not followed through. Somehow, writing it down as a "To Do," gives her a feeling of partial control over the problem. If that sounds far-fetched to you, try it on for size.

Let's go back to the question at the beginning of this chapter, and then the chapter title. Please reread the title—out loud. It's important. ENERGY comes before TIME. You see, we have time, plenty of it—in our days, in our evenings (quit your belly-aching and pity-partying—you know that if you *really* want to do something, you carve out the time for it). Isn't it amazing that the (often-times: self-proclaimed) "swamped" people always make it to the obligatory funerals? When you're tempted to sofa-crash at 6:30 PM, *time* is obviously not your problem. Your *energy* is drained.

Back to Tammie and her Wednesday. If she had *not* used **PHP**, she may *have*:

—yelled at her ten-year-old daughter for not laundering her own uniform..."You're not a baby, anymore, Sam!!" Energy drainer.

—ate leftover ice cream cake for breakfast... "Too damn busy to start that new healthy eating plan today." Energy drainer.

—called her "ex" and tell him to pick up the friggin' dog... "They're YOUR kids, you know!!" Energy drainer.

Okay, maybe it's slightly exaggerated. But maybe not. You may think, as many do, that "unloading" on people (even loved ones), helps get it out of you. After all, pent-up anger turns into hostility. Or worse yet, an emotional volcano. But yelling and anger simply become bad habits. An example of this is those managers that say they have to blow up every so often...or they'll burst! Once s/he realizes a good month or so has gone by, s/he'll DO IT. Let it out, baby—and not worry who's in the line of fire! And be sure about this too: those employees lucky enough to be present, will get it with both barrels! Not good.

It is no small task *not* to fall into this surprising trap. Old habits do indeed die hard. Bad habits cannot be stopped. They must be *replaced*— with **PHP**. People *don't* get rich quick. People *don't* lose forty pounds in a month. We can only hope to chip away. **PHP** is a process. The whale at Sea World *chips away.* Guess where the rope is in relation to the water, when some trainers teach him how to jump over it? No, guess again. Nope. It's on the ***bottom*** of the pool! The whale simply ***swims,*** and gets a fish! Before Shamu even knows it, the rope is many feet above the surface of the water. It's a process.

Let's end Tammie's day with her, shall we? It's home time now—kids' games, catch this, pop in at that. Life is simply a percolation of priorities. Energy control is like tuning a guitar—too much stress, strings break. Too little…'hardly plays. Preserving and conserving energy is not child's play. It requires focus—focus on the present—on what's going on right now! It requires **PHP.**

DIVERSITY: A GROWING NEED FOR TOLERANCE

We learned in grade school that approximately a century ago, America was a melting pot of nationalities. Presently there is a remelt materializing. There is no such thing as a typical American young person any more. The colors, accents, and cultural traditions are intermingled; hence *remelted.* Many conventional workers see this as difficulty…"Not the old way." Some managers just let it all be, believing that some old-schoolers just have engrained beliefs and should be left alone: "Everyone's entitled to their own opinion."

Yes and no. **PHP** Managers can instead choose to foster the means for remarkable learning experiences. Our workplaces are no longer blue-eyed and blonde-haired. Are employees entitled to their own opinions? Of course. But if **PHP** Managers enlighten traditional employees on the possibilities for *better*, the workplace can become stimulating! See how easy it may be to stimulate Buzz!

BUZZ: "Hey, hot shot—little boss man…"

MANAGER: "I'm assuming you're trying to get *my* attention, Buzz?"

BUZZ: "Yeah, whatever. I probably shouldn't call you that, but I never had a boss who didn't shave yet!"

MANAGER: "Yeah, I'm thinking of trying it. Maybe you could show me how. What's on your mind, Buzz? How can I help you?"

PHP Analysis Note: Survey the way this manager reacted to Buzz' sarcastic comment. He could have asked Buzz to give him the respect he deserves as the manager; or disregard it entirely, just moving on with the conversation; or *steer into the slide*, which is what you just read above. He mirrored Buzz' sarcasm, kept a straight face, as he felt it warranted neither laughter nor even a smile. Mirroring is not lowering oneself into the crater of mockery. It's merely acknowledging that you *get it*, but are choosing *not* to give it any future fuel of energy (no smile, *and* moving on deliberately with the conversation).

BUZZ: "It's the new Spanish guy. Dude is just so freakin' slow!"

MANAGER: "Jorge is actually as Spanish as you are, Buzz. He's originally from Guatemala. As far as I know, he's been an American citizen since he was four years old. I doubt he's ever been to Spain. I know all that from when we all introduced ourselves at the division meeting. With that hopefully cleared up for now, if you could expand on what you mean by *slow*, it may help me. The last productivity chart posted in the factory lounge showed his performance toward the top."

PHP Observation Note: Manager has totally used a neutral voice. This goes a long way. A defensive tone only encourages more walls to go up. Even if you feel like saying, "Buzz, you big, fat, hairy, smelly asshole of a bigot—who couldn't give a crap about anyone except yourself...who has mommy-issues and an ugly wife with whom you fathered ugly ki..." HOLD ON THERE Bubba-Boy (as Quick Draw McGraw used to say). Keep using the neutral voice—it helps set the mood for lowering "walls," which is your goal (***PATIENCE***).

BUZZ: "Whatever, I knew I couldn't talk to you."

MANAGER: (Remaining neutral in voice) "Please try to tell me what the real problem is, Buzz? (**PURITY**) You're a valuable person here. People like having you around. I feel a little helpless sometimes because you know your job so well (**HUMILITY**). What do you mean by Jorge being *slow?*"

(Remember the questioning technique…every conversation can progress with merely asking questions—in a non-accusatory, "pass-the-salt, please" manner).

BUZZ: "He just comes in, does his thing, don't say a thing to nobody!"

(**PAUSE**. Manager allows silence to enrich the communication. Some subscribe to the philosophy that the beginning of all progress begins with simple silence).

MANAGER: "Does he *ever* get involved in any break-time conversations? Talk about his family, his weekends?"

BUZZ: "Didn't even know he had a family. Just thought he was another Spanish guy in this countr…sorry, there I go again. I don't really know what the problem is. It's just that it used to just be us guys, then we have a couple chicks working on the floor too…then managers young enough to be our grandsons."

MANAGER: "I think I'm getting the jist of your concerns, Buzz. Change is a challenging thing to harness. We know what we have now; we don't know how it will be in the future. It's a little scary actually. I've seen my parents go through it too. Here's a suggestion, or maybe just a thought. You might try just sort of inviting Jorge into the fold a bit."

BUZZ: "Georgie knows he can hang with us; we don't do invitations on a silver platter around here."

MANAGER: "No, I mean more like to ask him about his family, his kids. The other employees you work with (and who respect you so much) will likely find Jorge has a lot of the same interests and problems that everyone else does. He's always wearing his White Sox hat."

BUZZ: "Can't hold that against him!" (Smiling, seeming to let down his guard a bit).

Maybe, *maybe* you have set some charitable wheels into motion. Maybe not. Embracing diversity is gradual, with go-aheads and set-backs (*PATIENCE*). Sometimes you'll have the answers, more often mere ideas (like the conversation above); sometimes you have nothin'! (*HUMILITY*). It's okay to share that too (*PURITY*). *Your* confidence and *your own* secure awareness, consciousness and philosophy of life—are attractive to your employees. In an uncertain world, people are starving to be led by **PHP** Managers who possess a secure, confident awareness of their surroundings. We (whoever we are) like being around people who know who they are, and where they are; on purpose. **PHP**.

SELF-MANAGING

Once upon a time, there was a baby-boomer manager named Cathleen. She had a good job, nice family, took night courses to better herself, cleaned her house on weekends, and scheduled time to shop with her 13-year-old daughter. She lived a tight schedule (and frankly frowned on those who did not). Cathleen stretched it, but if she kept her activities tight, with little compromise, everything functioned. She always brimmed with an atomic energy. Even her relaxing didn't seem relaxed. She tried walking, swimming, meditating—was always thinking and living in the next part of her day however. Even before the regular appointment of her blood pressure check (she had herself on an eight times a year schedule), she spent extra time on her rowing machine to de-stress as she was extra anxious pending what the reading would be.

Cathleen couldn't wait for Friday at 5:00 o'clock to come around; counted the days to vacation, and even retirement (1,682). She did not like change either. Life for Cathleen seemed to be a series of sighs and problems. Her employees mostly left her alone, as she rarely had time to chat. Not much MBWAing going on. Would *you* like to work with Cathleen?!

THIMK! *Stress is self-induced and self-fixed.*

But the self-fixing process is never over. Oh sure, we get pockets of fruition…"Whew, glad that project is over!" But change is constant. ACCEPT that. APPRECIATE it. It helps keep us on our toes, keeps us "thimking," keeps the weeds from growing around our feet. There are *always* better methods of doing almost anything! Only God is perfect. Remember goal *re-setting*? Life *is* a continuous percolation of priorities (for us *and* our employees). We leaders have the ability and obligation to teach, influence, and infect our students, families, customers…everyone!

ACTION BRIEF! *If the person you're visiting has their toilet paper roll going the wrong way (over or under to your preference), don't change it!*

Be open. Be flexible. Shoot holes in your own ideas before someone else does. If managers can tweak the small, relatively unimportant fragments of life, we can inch closer to the "big picture" of everything. And this my friends, is the place to be.

Recall a little throw-in line from the movie, Mr. Mom, where one reminds their spouse, how easy it is to forget the important things in life…"So don't." **PURITY, HUMILITY,** and **PATIENCE.** *Simple, focused thinking—in our complex world, will help to keep what is precious… on the front burners of our busy lives.*

Chapter 12

Bonus Section

STICKY LEGAL STUFF EVERY MANAGER AND SUPERVISOR SHOULD KNOW (BUT DIDN'T WANT TO ASK) SUCH AS:

"How deep can I really go, discussing her problems at home?"

"He said his outfit is for religious purposes, but it's spooking customers away!"

"Can I just outright ask her if she's pregnant?"

"Are you sure that's alcohol you smell on his breath?"

NOTES FROM THE PHP MANAGER'S JOURNAL...

"Ask. Ask again. Ask someone else. Ask, ask, and ask. You'll never find the answer in a text book. And if you ask two lawyers, you'll get four answers. Don't be embarrassed. Find a functioning, working supervisor who you respect and get their opinion. Find a couple of them for really confusing issues."

—J. G. *(prefers his initials be used), Restaurant Owner, NY*

CASE I:

"HOW DEEP CAN I REALLY GO, DISCUSSING HER PROBLEMS AT HOME?"

She's changed. No longer bubbly smiles. Still doing her job without complaints, but just doesn't seem happy. Sandra has only one son—the apple of her eye. All couple-dozen employees in her department (accounts payable in a large aerospace manufacturing corporation) saw Robbie grow up, as Sandy frequently brought him in to say hi. Everyone knew him as Robbie-Robot, his favorite nickname as a kid.

Sandy's smiles disappeared exactly two weeks ago. *No one* knows why. Her concerned fellow employees are asking *you* what's going on. You decide to have a private conversation with her.

MANAGER: "Hi, Sandy. How are you today?"

SANDY: "Okay, how are you?"

MANAGER: "I'm fine. Uhhm, not really sure how to start this conversation **(HUMILITY)** and I certainly don't want to pry **(PURITY)**, but many of us are concerned about you. You don't seem like your usual, happy self for the past couple weeks. (Sandy's eyes appear to be filling with emotion). Is everything okay?"

SANDY: (Able to compose herself in time to answer). "Everything is fine. Is that it? Cause I really have a lot of work to do."

(SANDY politely begins to rise, manager nods *sure*. Folded paper drops out of a folder she's carrying, manager sees it on the floor a few minutes after her departure. Not being sure if it was

Sandy's or belonging to someone else, manager opens the paper. The letterhead revealed the school district where Sandy lived. The seconds it took for the manager to realize it was personal business—was enough time to discover that Robbie-Robot quit school in the middle of his junior year).

Should the manager:

A. Leave it on Sandy's desk for her to find tomorrow morning? It's common for the cleaning people to pick stuff up off the floor as they're vacuuming.

B. Leave it on your office floor?

C. Call Sandy in, tell her you know and see what you can do to help?

D. Take her out to lunch; place it in front of her on her plate?

E. Google some stats how many dropouts make more money than many college grads?

F. Tell her many people at the company know or are even related to los…ahh, people who didn't finish high school?

Some thoughts of analysis follow. Notice there are pros and cons of each.

A. She may be less embarrassed not being confronted directly. At the same time, the suspense in the mystery of not knowing *who* found it could add stress to her situation.

B. If you leave it, she may come in "missing it," and just grab it off your floor (no harm, no foul…for you). Then again, *should* you be helping her more?

C. Are you prying? She may think so. Moreover, she may be mad you're going beyond your managerial boundaries (exactly the question—remember the title: "How deep can

I really go discussing her problems at home?") Then again, maybe she's just waiting for *some kind of help*.

D.   Nice thought, maybe a good idea; get her out of the office...but it may not be so nice if she begins balling in the restaurant.

E.   Believe it or not, this may help. Part of our human, inherent condition is that misery really does enjoy company. This may however, be better used as an after thought to another type of conversation. Think of this statistic as a "helpful PS."

F.   See "E" (above). But also take note of the poor attempt at humor in the original "F" option. She does feel like her precious little robot boy is a loser. She may feel like one as well.

THIMK! *If we knew the deep-down thoughts of the other guy—his heart, mind and gut...<u>really knew</u>, we would never have a bad thing to say about him/her. Ever.*

The **PHP** Manager recounted her words this way:

MANAGER: "Hi, Sandy. Sorry to call you back into the office; I know you said you have a lot to do. I found this on the floor— must have slipped out when you were in here. I opened it and before I even realized it was probably none of my business, I read it. (Short pause). In a way, it *is none* of my business, and I'm sorry (**HUMILITY**). In another way, I think the world of you and am glad to know what's been bothering you (**PURITY**). Not sure what if anything I can do to help, Sandy, but please let me know if I can."

(**SANDY** begins to cry, not uncontrollably, but with considerate, obvious pain. After 90 seconds, which seemed like 90 minutes, she simply walked out).

(Vital **PHP** Moment Analysis: You did what you thought you should. Your *inner sense* took charge. Now simply exercise ***PATIENCE***...*trust* in that inner sense),

> (**FOUR** Days Elapsed; Sandy sends the manager an e-mail requesting a short meeting. Again, by the **PHP** Manager's recount of the conversation, the dialogue follows):

SANDY: "Thanks for your time. I'm sorry I sobbed in the beginning of the week. I guess I just needed time to try to figure it all out. Since Bob died, Robbie has been my whole life. I was devastated when he told me he couldn't go another day to school. It's never been easy for him. After like second or third grade, it was always a struggle in the morning. He never had problems with other kids or anything like that. Teachers always liked him. Just didn't like school. (Sandy wipes away a passing tear, demonstrating growing composure). But over the past few weeks as I'm melting down, he seems happy. Happier than he's ever been. He got a job immediately with City-Wide Plumbing; has been there for over two weeks now. He washes his own uniforms, makes his own lunch, and leaves whistling in the morning in between saying *I love you, Mom!* (Tears flow, manager not sure why). It's like he... he...I don't know—found himself or something. (Pause; Sandy quite composed now). He even fixed my bathroom faucet leak— seems like it's been dripping for years! You got any leaks?! (Sandy and manager share a smile). Thanks for everything. (Pause). I think it's going to be okay." (Sandy leaves).

Soooo...what just happened? Appears that the **PHP** used by the manager in the original conversation payed off in some way. Sandy solved her own problem. Would she have *without* the conversation? It's anybody's guess. Point is, the more we can create a healthy, open, **PHP** environment for our employees, the more conducive it becomes for self-sticky-problem-solving. Employees have *inner senses* too. A **PHP** Manager's job includes nurturing it in all those around him/her.

CASE II:

"HE SAID HIS OUTFIT IS FOR RELIGIOUS PURPOSES, BUT IT'S SPOOKING CUSTOMERS AWAY!"

No one has yet complained, but the eye-brow-raised glance you received from the regular customer as she left the restaurant— spoke volumes. Timone was a great worker. Still is, actually. But what's up with his new matching hat and gown? Sure, he still wears his mandatory apron, but it almost disappears in those vibrant colors of his...*costume?* Not your word, but one actually ushered in under an employee's breath to another. You almost wish you hadn't heard it. (Note: there is no other dress code but the apron at this casual restaurant).

So, you do what every good **PHP** Manager does. You wait. You watch. You listen. All seemed okay. Tuesday night: business as usual. But Wednesday evening, Timone mentioned to you that his tips were "off." That Friday, *you* noticed the *amount per customer* was considerably down—only for Timone's tables. Do you:

A. "Give him enough slack" and he'll discover he's decreasing his own bread-and butter-take-home? Like, he'll figure it out when it hits 'em in the fanny pack?

B. Tell him at the end of the night he looks like a clown and cut the crap?

C. Encourage the employees to kind of surround him— intervention style, and tell him to straighten out his act?

D. Pay one of *your* friends to eat in the place and tell the waiter (Timone) that he (customer) does not feel comfortable being waited on by a "religious geek" and is not getting a tip?

E. Call his mom (he's almost 30)?

Believe it or not, it's likely that most of the above seem like valuable options to you. But let's just cut to the **PHP** chase on this one, shall we? Hopefully (by this chapter), you don't even think B, D, and E are good ones. And though C could work in a close knit joint—where there are shared gratuities, and so on…this isn't the situation in this restaurant.

So back to A. If he spooks away enough customers (and let's be honest), yes, it could happen…he may decide his ability to eat and put gas in his vehicle trumps religious expression. All well and good for him. But not you. Whatever is your image, it's *your image*. There's a certain culture in every establishment. Culture, we learn in Sociology determines what is good, what is true, and what is beautiful. There's a culture in your company; there's a culture in your church; there's a culture in your poker group; a culture in your home. You get the picture. You, **PHP** Manager, are in charge of maintaining that… culture in your workplace, for that's the "stuff" that makes your cash register ring.

> **MANAGER:** "Hi, Timone, I just need a couple minutes of your time. We can grab this corner over here…"

(Analytical **PHP** Pause on "Setting:" You remember "setting" when you did a book report in third grade. It meant *time and place*. **PHP** Managers should be conscious of setting. And that does not mean always in the office—where "everyone knows something's going on." Some of the best-results-conversations have transpired in parking lots, trains, even public rest rooms. So here we are back in the corner of the restaurant…)

(**PHP** Reminder Note: Always follow the advice of your HR department and/or the policies and procedures of your company. It's the best way to insure fairness and consistency with your employees. That being said, if a behavior like dress code is affecting sales and profits, it becomes a BFOQ—*bona-fide occupational qualification*: that an employee conform to what has worked historically in the company to maintain that level of profitability).

MANAGER: "I'm not sure how to start this conversation, or frankly—I grappled with whether I even should broach it (**HUMILITY**). But I came to the conclusion that if it were me, I would want my manager to bring it up (**PURITY**). And also, I'm concerned that it's going to affect business. I'm referring to the way you're dressing lately. First I thought it was just your business, but I'm afraid it could actually hurt sales (**PURITY, HUMILITY**). I realize you've mentioned that it has to do with your new religious practices—and I/we totally respect that. Sooo, I'm hoping that by just bringing it to your attention that your 'amount per customer' has been down consistently since it started, maybe you had an idea how to address it." (**PATIENCE**).

TIMONE: "I don't know what to say?" (Long pause)

MANAGER: "Okay, well…thanks for your time. (Pause). Maybe, I guess we can both just think about it all."

Manager definitely used the **PHP** principles. You recall that a major part of using the *inner sense* is that both the problem and the solution seem to take on a life of their own. Meaning that you (**PHP** Manager) are not in full control of the outcome. Your goal of course, is to have a restaurant flowing with happy, healthy workers and generous, returning customers. *How* you get there and stay there—is not written in stone.

Fast forward to Timone's next shift, two days after the conversation; he arrived in his typical khakis, sport shirt, and apron (just like the old days). Business as usual. Never another conversation was had. The dollar numbers rose back up to normal levels. Is it really that easy? Can it honestly work like that?! Yes. Not always, but often. The key **PHP** Management TTD (thing to do) here is to APPRECIATE how it all turned out—and not slack off in that APPRECIATION. For tomorrow's a new day—with new problems to be solved or re-solved.

CASE III:

"Can I just outright ask her if she's pregnant?!"

Chelsea is the best employee in your deli. Can do everything—cook, cater, counter—everything you can do. She's paid well, never any issues nor drama; possibly because she's also rather private in her personal affairs. When she took a week vacation last spring, she came back married. The only way people knew was by the ring on her finger, and a phone message left by her "husband." You congratulated her, she said, thanks, and it was back to work.

You have a big decision to make. A local country club asked you to be their exclusive caterer this coming summer. Chelsea would be a major player in this. But it's October, and she's looking a bit fuller in the midsection. Could she be with child? November, December, Janu… that would put her in baby-land around…July! Holy mackerel! For this new catering gig, could you ever do it without her? You need to know as you have to sign the contract soon. You ask her, "Chelsea, are you guys planning to have kids?" You even phrased the question so as not to mention her weight gain. But the answer still stumped you.

She smiles and says, "You know better than to ask me that." Now what?! The healthy **PHP** common-sense rule to live by reads something like this: If personal behaviors and/or circumstances of our employees get in the way of doing business (directly or indirectly), it *is* our business.

The manager subscribed to the aforementioned dogma; then proceeded to **PHP** his way through the issue. His foolproof *inner sense* yielded this conversation.

> MANAGER: "Chelsea, I didn't mean to pry into your personal business the other day—asking you about your future family plans. Fact is, we have this opportunity for catering with the Agotok Country Club and I believe we could handle it with you still being here this summer. Not asking for an employment contract, nor do I need to know your personal plans. Honestly,

I'm just not sure what to do about the decision." (The last sentence alone is packed full of **PURITY, HUMILITY,** and **PATIENCE**). "*If* chances are fairly good you'll still be here, I'd like to go for it. If there's some strong possibilities for whatever reason—you may *not* be working here, I'll likely turn it down. You're a big part of our whole business here." (Pause).

CHELSEA: (Somewhat sarcastically) "So you want to know if I have one in the oven…"

MANAGER: "I don't seem to be doing a good job of communicating here. So maybe we should just stop talking for now—maybe another time. Like I said, I'm just not certain what to do about the decision I need to make." (Manager walks away).

Why was Chelsea acting so weird, and even a little defensively? Remember **PHP**ers—*it doesn't matter.* You have done the right thing; relied upon your powerful *inner sense,* drawn through you and for you by your being **PURE, HUMBLE,** and **PATIENT**. You "put it out there." Now wait.
(**PHP** Note of Understanding: This is one of the toughest parts—for you cannot control this next sequence of events. The issue has taken on a life of its own. You'll know if/when you'll need to say or do anything else. Just wait. **PATIENCE** is truly a virtue).

ACTION BRIEF! Get excited about not knowing every little detail of what's behind the next door!

(8:35 PM that same evening): Chelsea calls manager, quickly but conversationally states "she'll be around." They are having a baby, and they're looking forward to it all, and her husband will be starting to work from home all summer. Baby's due beginning of June, and other than shortening her hours, but *increasing her days;* she'll be fully on board for July and August (crucial catering months). She is excited about Agotok and loves working with you. (After a brief pause, added) "The reason I freaked out a bit was when I was 19, I became pregnant, and the owner of the restaurant where I worked politely told me (as soon as he found out) that that night would be my last. Sorry I put you in that category. You didn't deserve it."

(**PHP** PS. Was the restaurateur previously mentioned within his rights to can the mother-to-be? BFOQ, bona-fide occupational qualification, says *maybe*. If the business may/will suffer financially, and it can be shown, demonstrated, proven by the business owner/manager…yes, it's legal discrimination. No sarcasm intended, but there are not too many pregnant pole dancers. And maybe a pregnant nurse wouldn't be the best person to be working at an abortion clinic where lots of emotions create even more challenges for the patients. This kind of thinking may not be pleasant, but is valid and needed in effective employee relations).

CASE IV:

"ARE YOU SURE THAT'S ALCOHOL YOU SMELL ON HIS BREATH?"

Ron arrived back from lunch a bit later than usual. His speech seemed slurred. Was he wobbling or was that your imagination? You walked closely to his workspace at his cashiering station. Just as you figured—alcohol on his breath! When you asked him how was lunch, he just laughed and said bug off—"I gots custuuuuumuuuz to ranggg!" Why he slipped into this accent puzzled you. One of your fellow managers at the large home furnishings store whispered to you, "Fire his ass, he's always been strange." Another employee, a Big-Mouth-Millie type (remember her from Chapter Three?) coached you, "I don't know why you put up with that crap from anyone!" One of your security folks chimed in, "You let one get hammered at lunch, you're gonna' have biiig problems!"

You knew you had to remove the immediate "dangers" from a safety standpoint, a customer service standpoint, and a legal standpoint. You escorted Ron into the stockroom. Didn't make it any easier that he was poking your chest by this time, while introducing you to a few, new four-letter words. You instructed Ron that two store security people (one male, one female) would escort him home. The emergency number you had on record connected you to a concerned but not surprised sister, who thanked you and said she would meet him there at home.

Immediate situation under control. But you felt an incredible pressure to fire the bum. **PATIENCE**, my friend. And with all the supervising courses you've had, you'd think you'd know exactly how to handle Ron now. Embracing your **HUMILITY**, you simply *don't* know. You feel like caving into peer pressure (remember high school?) and terminating him. You'll be revered then! Feared even!! But in your heart of hearts (AKA your deep gut), you'd be lying to yourself if you believed it was the best next-step strategy (**PURITY**).

So you wait. Next day, Ron's sister leaves a message that he's okay, resting comfortably. You're obviously thinking hangover. But two days later, it's your move (your cronies tell you so!). But you wait **PATIENTLY**, for you still don't know what to do (**HUMILITY**). And then among your clouds of confusion, at quarter past four in the afternoon, there he is—gracing your office door.

MANAGER: "Hi, Ron."

RON: "Hi, got a few? (Manager still unsure of what is to come but somewhat relieved that *something* is happening, signals a warm gesture for Ron to come in and sit down). I know you probably wanted to can my fat ass, and I wouldn't have thought any less o' ya if you did. But thanks for not, and getting me home safely and all that other stuff, whatever it was; cause I don't even remember—hardly any of it. (Ron alternating making eye contact among you, the papers on the desk, and his hands in his lap) I actually have a type of sugar diabetes—something which makes me appear drunk—including how I smell like it during the episode. Doesn't happen more than a couple times every ten years or so. Should have told you when I started. But that's why they let me go from Evergreen Electronics. They thought I was a rummy. Fact is, I don't drink at all. (Ron pauses for his sake, not yours—meaning that he's quite focused on his monologue). Doc says if I do certain things at certain times, I can control these fits. So I will, I promise. So if it's okay, I'll just come back to work tomorrow. And if you don't mind, if we can keep it between us, I'd appreciate it."

MANAGER: "Thanks for sharing all this, Ron. Other than copying the VP of HR, and my boss, Regina—just because she's the store manager, no…I'll tell no one. They'll see you have it under control."

(**PHP** Manager's Guide to Confidentiality "Tidbit:" If you're human, you can't wait to hop on the horn right away, and begin your conversation with "You're not going to believe what I heard. YOU CAN'T TELL ANYONE though…" This is the kiss of communication death. The "need to know" (not!) grapevine sluts and gossip whores will have a field day with this). You have a few choices:

One) Say absolutely nothing. If anyone has the audacity to ask (and they will), politely say it's not their business. This only thickens the plot.

Two) When people ask, simply say something to the effect that it's all fixed, everything's cool. Most will not be satisfied with this, and will keep looking.

Three) This is recommended and probably should be *cleared* with Ron prior to doing it. "Good morning, everyone. Brought you all here for a very brief, but important announcement. You're all obviously familiar with the incident with Ron Tuesday morning. I am glad to share that everything is okay with Ron. He'll be back to work tomorrow. Thanks for not asking me any additional questions, because I can't and won't share any more. But I wanted you all to know the good news for one of our fellow employees to prevent any speculating around the office. That's it. Thanks again. Have a great day everyone."

Most will respect your request—and subtly but powerfully, you have made a serious premium deposit in their "trust insurance policies" in you. They know…if and when something embarrassing happened to them/ with them, you would somehow handle it professionally and comfortably for all involved.

END NOTE...

Spiders navigate sticky situations for a living. Bugs get stuck all the time, but spiders maneuver smoothly and easily. How do they do it? Some say they secrete an anti-stick oil, but no one knows for sure. They DO try to stay on the drier parts of the web, to avoid the gluey parts. But they actually can walk across the stickiest parts of their webs. Biologists tell us they have evolved with a third claw on their feet which somehow moves the sticky strands out of the way to permit the spider to cross their own webs—but still leaving them sticky to catch their prey.

What the heck does this have to do with us...managing people? We need to become more and more comfortable navigating across sticky employee-situation "webs." You have a third claw too—your PHP. As the fascinating spider has evolved, so will you; to become a fine manager—a prized value. For those who can handle prickly communication people issues, efficiently, smoothly and effectively, are in a species very high up in the food chain of life.

ABOUT THE
AUTHOR

TIM McHEFFEY brings over thirty years of being on the "firing-line" daily, demonstrating solutions to true-to-life, excruciatingly-painful workplace problems with employees. McHeffey has worked with both large and small companies, profit and not-for-profit. He is a past seminar-author and presented for both SkillPath and Dun and Bradstreet, and has successfully trained thousands of business people. Tim resides in Center Moriches, NY with his wife, Danielle. He has four children.

His publications include:

Juggling the Journey... Thirty-five Keys to Effective Living (at work and home). IBE, NY 1996.
>—It was on this book that he based his Dun and Bradstreet seminar, Self-Management, rolled out in cities throughout California in 1999.

Maintaining the Store...Keeping Up Appearances. Crisp Learning, CA 2003
>—used in corporate training programs at Williams-Sonoma, Pottery Barn and Hold Everything.

Dealing With Difficult Customers. Mark-Ed, OH 2005
>—used in classrooms across America to help students communicate more effectively when dealing with the public.

AND THAT'S NOT ALL!

*...As a very special **thank you** for investing in this book and mastering **Solving YOUR Sticky People Problems,** we invite you to go to:*

www.solvingstickypeopleproblems.com

CLICK ON: *"Hey, Tim! I'm ready for my book bonus!"*
When it prompts for SECRET CODE (*Shhhhh...*), put in "PHP"

You'll receive a thirty-minute, video-highlights-version of a live workshop, where Tim and a half-dozen of his closest manager-friends demyth and debunk some of the most prickly employee issues. The powerful, full-three-hour, workshop-video-course will be released in 2012 for $497 (complete with follow-along workbooklet)...
but the "highlights" version is *YOURS...NOW...FREE...for being one of the very first readers of **Solving Sticky People Problems!***

PS. While you're on the site, be sure to leave your e-mail address for monthly "Stick-E" Updates!
Also, take the four-question test to see if you're a *Black N' White Cookie Manager,* a *Wishy-Washy-Wet-Dish-Rag Manager,* a *Tight-Rope-Walker Manager,* or a ***PHP Manager!***

INDEX

A

B

C

D

E

G

H

I

J

L

BUY A SHARE OF THE FUTURE IN YOUR COMMUNITY

These certificates make great holiday, graduation and birthday gifts that can be personalized with the recipient's name. The cost of one S.H.A.R.E. or one square foot is $54.17. The personalized certificate is suitable for framing and will state the number of shares purchased and the amount of each share, as well as the recipient's name. The home that you participate in "building" will last for many years and will continue to grow in value.

Here is a sample SHARE certificate:

HABITAT FOR HUMANITY

THIS CERTIFIES THAT
YOUR NAME HERE
HAS INVESTED IN A HOME FOR A DESERVING FAMILY

1985-2005
TWENTY YEARS OF BUILDING FUTURES IN OUR
COMMUNITY ONE HOME AT A TIME

1200 SQUARE FOOT HOUSE @ $65,000 = $54.17 PER SQUARE FOOT
This certificate represents a tax deductible donation. It has no cash value.

YES, I WOULD LIKE TO HELP!

I support the work that Habitat for Humanity does and I want to be part of the excitement! As a donor, I will receive periodic updates on your construction activities but, more importantly, I know my gift will help a family in our community realize the dream of homeownership. **I would like to SHARE in your efforts against substandard housing in my community!** *(Please print below)*

PLEASE SEND ME _____ SHARES at $54.17 EACH = $ $_____

In Honor Of: _____

Occasion: (Circle One)   HOLIDAY   BIRTHDAY   ANNIVERSARY

    OTHER: _____

Address of Recipient: _____

Gift From: _____ *Donor Address:* _____

Donor Email: _____

I AM ENCLOSING A CHECK FOR $ $_____ PAYABLE TO HABITAT FOR HUMANITY **OR** PLEASE CHARGE MY VISA OR MASTERCARD *(CIRCLE ONE)*

Card Number _____ Expiration Date: _____

Name as it appears on Credit Card _____ Charge Amount $ _____

Signature _____

Billing Address _____

Telephone # Day _____ Eve _____

PLEASE NOTE: Your contribution is tax-deductible to the fullest extent allowed by law.
Habitat for Humanity • P.O. Box 1443 • Newport News, VA 23601 • 757-596-5553
www.HelpHabitatforHumanity.org

CPSIA information can be obtained at www.ICGtesting.com
Printed in the USA
BVOW061718110512

289749BV00001B/5/P